The Black History Truth: Argentina

'Aquí no hay negroes- There are no Blacks here'

Pamela Gayle

Grosvenor House
Publishing Limited

All rights reserved
Copyright © Pamela Gayle, 2021

The right of Pamela Gayle to be identified as the author of this
work has been asserted in accordance with Section 78
of the Copyright, Designs and Patents Act 1988

The book cover is copyright to Pamela Gayle

This book is published by
Grosvenor House Publishing Ltd
Link House
140 The Broadway, Tolworth, Surrey, KT6 7HT.
www.grosvenorhousepublishing.co.uk

This book is sold subject to the conditions that it shall not, by way of
trade or otherwise, be lent, resold, hired out or otherwise circulated
without the author's or publisher's prior consent in any form of binding or
cover other than that in which it is published and
without a similar condition including this condition being imposed
on the subsequent purchaser.

A CIP record for this book
is available from the British Library

ISBN 978-1-83975-525-5

Grosvenor House
Publishing Limited

External website links are provided for informational and educational purposes only. The links were accurate, reliable and relevant at the time of publication. The author accepts no liability or responsibility for any content on the linked sites and does not endorse or guarantee any of the information found on external links. Neither does the author exercise any control over the content of externally linked websites. Any comments or inquiries regarding the linked websites provided or their content should be directed solely to the owners of those websites.

Excerpts reproduced with kind courtesy and permission from:
American Economic Association, Cambridge University Press, Copyright Clearance Centre, Duke University Press, Historical Reflections John Hopkins University Press, Journal of Southern History, New York Historical Society, PLS clear, Sage Publications, Taylor & Francis, University of Arizona Press, University of North Carolina at Chapel Hill Libraries, University of Minnesota Press, Graduate School of Vanderbilt University, Yale Representation Limited, Yale University Press, Western Washington University.

Every effort has been made to trace copyright holders for the use of material in this book. The author apologises for any errors or omissions herein. Please contact the author for notification of any corrections that should be incorporated in future reprints or editions of this book. Image credits and permission provided in this book constitutes an extension of this copyright notice.

Dedication

In memory of my father, who recently passed away. Time may soften the blow, but your memory won't fade.

To a wonderful young man, loving and strong and kind, – my son.

To Dave, Veronica, Nadia, Jacqui and Myrtle for their encouragement and support.

International Decade for People of African descent 2015-2024 proclaimed by the UN General Assembly

The Black History Truth: Argentina
'Aquí no hay negroes- There are no Blacks here'

Introduction: The Black History Truth: Argentina
'Aquí no hay negroes' - *There are no Blacks here*

This book has been written to:
- provide a visual glimpse into the Black presence in Argentina up to the end of the nineteenth century
- close the gap caused by *historia negra negada* (denied Black history) and the sanitised view of colonialism
- stimulate and motivate interest in the Black History Truth for everyone within a specific geographical region

As this provides a short introduction, it is hoped that young people will find the contents stimulating enough to further their Black History education, and become empowered as a result of their knowledge and understanding. It is hoped that adults will read this introductory book and share their knowledge. It is further hoped that educators find this book useful as a resource.

This book explores the presence of Black people in Argentina. It is an overview of the historical root cause of, *'aquí no hay negroes'*. Each page starts with a question or query; focusses on a theme; and includes visuals to inspire, with brief explanations that are reviewed or critiqued using expert secondary sources. Some of the images, documents used and quotes are primary sources. Included also are guidelines for those who are nervous or unsure of how to approach this subject, together with approaches to the activities.

Most historical sources and illustrations were written and drawn by upper class white men who were royals, conquistadors, slavers, officials, missionaries, explorers and traders. Such sources, contain the "cultural arrogance" of the Eurocentric viewpoint. Whilst it is important not to bring modern attitudes to the past, Eurocentric perspectives should be kept in mind because it ignores and distorts African and Indian peoples' history. Whilst at the same time, revealing factual information as well as their attitudes and perceptions.

Argentina had historical links with the Angolan kingdom of Ndongo and Kongo; located in West Central Africa and where most of the enslaved came from. Captives also came from Guinea, Mozambique via U.S. or Portuguese slaving vessels. By the end of the nineteenth century, Black people were considered part of the 'disappeared past', and the Indian peoples 'defeated and exterminated'. It should be further borne in mind that, contemporary or historical sources were written mainly in Spanish and Portuguese, but research in English has been undertaken, whilst others sources have been translated. Today, Black people in Argentina are called Afro-Argentines.

Guidelines to follow

1. Avoid role plays and dramas as these may cause distress, embarrassment or defensiveness.
2. Avoid using videos or images of atrocities, as they may demean the victims.
3. Avoid the 'feeling sorry for blacks' or 'poor blacks versus horrible whites'.
4. Avoid generalisations, as not 'all blacks' nor 'all whites' experiences are the same.
5. Avoid narrowing the slavery trade without relating it to the legacy of wider contemporary issues.
6. Avoid comparisons that modern human trafficking is as bad or worse or the same.
7. Avoid comparisons of attitudes between other historical periods *(for instance, women were seen as physically, mentally, emotionally, and morally inferior to men, and many women believed this; punishments were cruel according to today's standards)*
8. Avoid the false equivalence of indentured or bonded labour, involuntary servitude or immigration.
9. Avoid learning about the European slave trade only during Black History Month.
10. Avoid projecting what you think is the 'correct' emotional response but acknowledge that there may be times when it is uncomfortable.
11. Avoid treating individuals as if they represent an entire racial group.
12. Avoid the association of whiteness with purity, goodness, innocence, power and superiority.
13. Avoid the association of blackness with difficulty, danger, death, criminality, and evil. Examples below are so rooted in everyday language that associated racist origins have long been forgotten.

Black cloud	Black mark	Black sheep	Blacklist	Black hole	Black out	Black spot
Black leg	Black heart	Black economy	Black market	Black cat	Black death	Black eye
Blackmail	Black and blue	Black magic	Black day	Black books	Black widow	Blackball

Focus on and celebrate the strength of the human spirit

How to approach the activities

Each page has a theme and activities which deepen and widen interest even further. Activities are placed at the end of every chapter. This book can be read from cover to cover without attempting any of the activities. Or, just read or complete any activity of interest. The following might be useful to think about.

1. Identify unconscious or conscious biases.
2. Identify where biases overlap and intersect such as age, gender, race, nationality, ethnicity and class.
3. Identify any misconceptions reguarly and provide time for reflection and self awareness.
4. Identify and define key words and phrases in order to gain confidence about the topic.
5. Identify the titles as key questions or queries to focus on throughout.
6. Identify occupations that can be further explored such as historian, archaeologist, anthropologist, biologist
7. Identify the historic timeline, and or events in other parts of the world within the same era.
8. Identify films, video clips, images and media, for age and level appropriateness and suitability before use.
9. Identify critical character traits such as perseverance and determination that can overcomes challenges.
10. Idenitfy how respect for human rights has evolved.
11. Understanding is the key rather than persuasion.
12. Follow the guidelines.

Remember, there is always a reason why things are the way they are

Contents

	Introduction	vi
	Guidelines to follow	vii
	How to approach the activities	viii

Chapter 1	*Where is Argentina?*	1
	What has silver got to do with it?	2
	How big is Argentina?	3
	What are the national symbols of Argentina?	4
	What are the main biomes in Argentina?	5
	How are the natural features in danger?	6
	Chapter 1 Activities	7

Chapter 2	*Without Indians, there are no Americas*	9
	Who were the Patagonian Giants?	10
	Who were Argentina's invaders?	11
	In God and encomienda, we trust?	12
	How did Indians avoid encomienda?	13
	Were the Jesuit Missions an earthly paradise?	14
	Chapter 2 Activities	15

Chapter 3	*What is the legacy of the Kongo Kingdom?*	17
	Why was the Kongo Princess burned at the stake?	18
	Could diamonds be forever?	19
	What was the Assiento de Negroes?	20
	To raid or not to raid; is that the question?	21
	What is the fallacy of Africans selling each other?	22
	What is the fallacy of Africans selling each other 2?	23
	Floating tombs – a way to die?	24
	What is the evidence of chattel enslavement?	25
	Chattel enslavement activities	26
	How many were raced across the Atlantic?	27
	Who was sold to the highest bidder?	28
	Chapter 3 Activities	29-30

Chapter 4	*What was the Spanish invention of racism?*	32
	Who was white but not quite?	33
	How to buy whiteness and be perfectly white	34
	How the castas divided and controlled	35
	How African blood is triumphant	36
	What was the myth of Black violence?	37
	What were Piezas de Indias?	38
	Chapter 4 Activities	39-40

Chapter 5	*Who were the gauchos and what did they invent?*	42	
	Why was the bottomless bucket misappropriated?	43	
	What was the Tasajo slavery trail to Cuba?	44	
	There weren't any plantations here…	45	
	What was the cycle of low status labour?	46	
	How fashionable were Black children?	47	
	Chapter 5 Activities	48	

Chapter 6	*How did the enslaved resist?*	50
	What were the mutiny myths?	51
	What were the white myths of resistance?	52
	What were the white abolition myths?	53
	How the Blacks *has* kill'd the whites…	54
	Is the price of manumission freedom?	55
	Free or freed or freeborn or free slave?	56
	What is the myth of the slave house?	57
	Chapter 6 Activities	58-59

Chapter 7	*Why did the British invade?*	61
	What is the 20bn bailout to slave-owning Brits?	62
	Why is an Argentine an Italian who speaks Spanish and thinks he's British?	63
	Was it conquest of the desert or genocide?	64
	In the name of the tourist gaze…	65
	Chapter 7 Activities	66

Chapter 8	*Why is Argentina known as the whitest nation?*	68
	What was the blanqueamiento of Black people?	69
	Why was the Black Mother of Argentina forgotten?	70
	How were the enslaved rescued?	71
	Who was the real El Negro Falucho?	72
	Chapter 8 Activities	73

Chapter 9	*What is the Candombe dance?*	75
	How and why did tango change colour?	76
	Who were the payadores and what are pulperias?	77
	From slave food to national dish…	78
	How to serve the drink of the gods	79
	Chapter 9 Activities	80

United Nations Human Rights Reports	82
Glossary	83
References 1,2,3,4	84, 85, 86, 87
Picture and Quote Credits	88
Index	89
Author	90

Chapter 1

Where is Argentina?	1
What has silver got to do with it?	2
How big is Argentina?	3
What are the national symbols?	4
What are the main biomes in Argentina?	5
How are the natural features in danger?	6
Chapter 1 Activities	7

Figure 1: World continents map showing South America in purple and Africa in orange

Where is Argentina?

In the South American continent. It is the fourth largest continent in the world and the second largest country after Brazil. Chile and the Andes Mountains borders the west side. Argentina is known as the 'Whitest Nation in South America'.

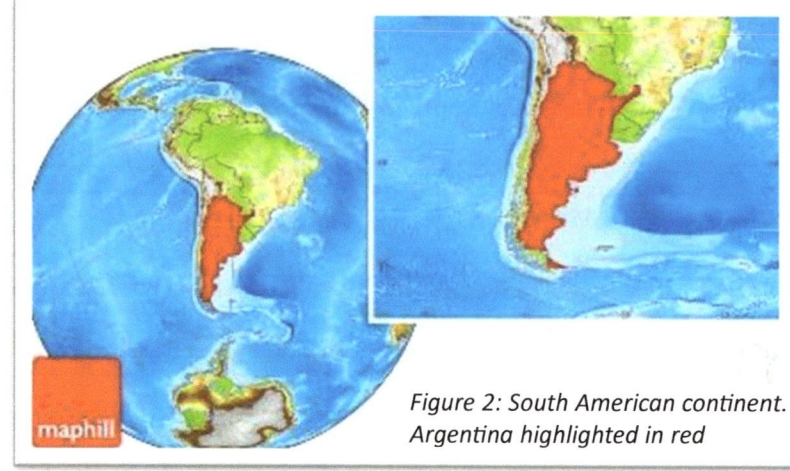

Figure 2: South American continent. Argentina highlighted in red

Argentina lies between the Atlantic and Pacific Oceans in the southern hemisphere and is an inverted triangular in shape. It lies mostly on the bottom half of the South American continent. Spanish is the official language and English is taught in most schools. *Lunfardo* is the African language mainly mixed with Spanish, Italian and Portuguese. Guarani and Quechua are official Indian languages in the Corrientes province.

Figure 3: Watch the Continental Drift Video: See Chapter 1 Activities

Alfred Wegener, a nineteenth century geologist, thought that all the continents were one big land mass called Pangaea, because South America's east coast fitted into the west coast of Africa like a jigsaw puzzle with similar geographies and climates. The continents split about 150 million years ago, according to some experts. Although plate tectonics has taken over that notion today.

On the Atlantic Ocean side is the 180-mile-long Río de la Plata river. Río de la Plata means Silver River in English. This is where the first arrivals of enforced Africans landed, either in 1534 or in 1587. Before 1587, captives went overland to Potosi in Bolivia as silver mine labourers, a journey of nearly three thousand km from Río de la Plata. However, '...more than 13,000 Negroes valued at 1,479,441 silver pesos were imported into Buenos Aires, from 1586 to 1655...' according to African American anthropologist Irene Diggs in 1951.

More recent studies of Spanish, Argentine and Portuguese archives by Historian, Dr Kara Schultz in 2015, calculated that '...at least **34,224** Africans were landed in Buenos Aires on 253 voyages between 1587 and 1640.' They came mainly from the Kongo and Ndongo Kingdoms in Angola, West Central Africa and from Brazil. The Spanish needed their African skills to build empires as they were already experts in mining for salt, gold and copper; producing metal work, trade and trading as well as experienced in large-scale agriculture.

The truth is that Argentina gained immense wealth from the African enslaved; their skills helped to develop Argentina's wealth in agriculture and livestock by the mid nineteenth century. Today, Argentina is known for its meat industries and economies. Nonetheless, as Argentina wanted a white history, Africans' contributions to nation building was subjected to *historia negra negada*.

What has silver got to do with it?

Historians say that America was named after the explorer Amerigo Vespucci who was a conquistador for Spain. He arrived on the continent in 1502. His arrival, together with the Spanish invaders that followed, led to devastating events for the people already living there. Devastating for the Indians and devastating for the Africans forcibly taken to Argentina.

The Spanish invaded in 1516 and called the country 'Argentum because they found silver in the river', claimed *Encyclopaedia Britannica*. Argentum is Latin for silver. At first, they were after the legendary city of silver called Sierra de la Plata (Mountain of Silver). Instead, their desire for precious metals led them inland to the silver mines of Potosi, Bolivia. Eventually, the Spanish colonised the Río de la Plata region. They ruled for over three hundred years.

Buenos Ayres is a port city. The people were known as 'porteños'. Before 1770s, the city had 'a wild and unfinished look about it, which is anything but pleasing', wrote explorer Samuel Haigh (1817). Only useful due to its location on the Atlantic Ocean with overland routes to Potosi.

By the nineteenth century, the area was called Buenos Ayres meaning 'Good Airs' or "Fair Winds". Previously, the air stank with the terrible stench of slaughtered cattle and salted meats. When meat began to be refrigerated, the air smelt better and therefore named, *Santa María del Buen Ayre,* (Buenos Ayres). Or, as suggested by some historians, Buenos Ayres meant 'favourable winds that guided ships to the port'. The city became Argentina's capital in 1880.

The 180-mile-long Río de la Plata river separates Argentina from Uruguay. Both the Uruguay and Paraná rivers flow together before meeting in the Atlantic Ocean. This forms the estuary of the Río de la Plata, which often floods, leaving sediment to be cleared to keep the port open. According to University history Professor Dr Alex Borucki's research, a total of **70,225** enslaved were imported between 1777 and 1812 to the banks of the Río de la Plata.

Figure 4: Río de la Plata River from the sky, showing sediment

Figure 5: Buenos Aires from above. 1860 approximately

How big is Argentina?

Argentina shares land borders with five other countries. One of those countries is Brazil, where many of the enslaved came from. Before 1816, it was known as the Viceroyalty of the Río de la Plata, or just Río de la Plata (from the name of the river), and after 1816 as United Provinces of the Río de la Plata. In 1776, Río de la Plata comprised parts of Argentina, parts of Uruguay, Paraguay, and Bolivia. Enslavement was officially abolished in 1861. It became Argentine Republic in 1862.

Today, Argentina is divided into five regions with **23 provinces**. Each province has its own flag and officials, with Buenos Aires (Ayres) as the capital today. Argentina is immense. The land area is about **2,800,000 km²** including Patagonia, and is the second largest country in South America. Compare this to the United Kingdom's land area of only **243,000 km²** approximately.

Figure 6: 1820s map showing Río de la Plata in orange. Included parts of Uruguay and Bolivia

Argentina is the **eighth** largest country in the world and **eleven** times bigger than the UK. The United Kingdom is the **78th** largest. Argentina's current population is about **45,000,000** as of 2020, whereas the UK's population is about **67,800,000** as of 2020. The population density is **17** people every km² and UK is **281** people every km². Life expectancy is about **82** years in UK and **77** years in Argentina.

Argentina is located in the Southern Hemisphere, below the equator. UK is in the Northern Hemisphere, above the equator. When it's summer in the Northern Hemisphere, its winter time in the Southern Hemisphere. Buenos Ayres is warmer than London at nearly **4,000** km from the equator, whereas London is nearly **6,000** km away and therefore, cooler than Buenos Aires.

Argentina's land area is so immense that there are different climate zones from one region to another. In the north, it is nearly tropical, because it is nearer the equator. In the middle, the climate is temperate, similar to the UK. Below Patagonia, in the far south, is the Tierra del Fuego, which is a group of islands where the temperature ranges from minus 10°C to minus 55°C. It is the coldest and iciest region, nearest Antarctica.

Figure 7: Map of Regions and Provinces

What are the national symbols of Argentina?

Figure 8: Flag of Argentina

The flag was made in 1812 with three wide horizontal stripes. The white stripe may stand for the silver found in the river when the Spanish invaded. The blue may represent the waters of Argentina's Río de la Plata, where the enslaved were unloaded. The sun, added in 1818, is the Sol de Mayo and stands for the Inca sun god Inti, in the Incan tradition. Or the sun represents the rising of a new nation when Río de la Plata and Patagonia joined together to form Argentina.

Figure 10: Erythrina crista-galli: National flower of Argentina.

The Erythrina crista-galli is the national flower, known as Ceibo in Spanish, or Cockspur coral in English. It grows wild in swamps and wetlands and is known for its bright red flowers. The red colour represents bravery for the Indian peoples, according to this legend.

LEGEND: Story of Anahi, a young Guarani speaking woman. She was captured by Spanish conquistadors, but killed her capturers when she was trying to escape. Anahi fled into the forest only to be captured again. She was tied to a tree and burned alive as punishment. When the conquistadors returned for her body, they discovered a cockspur coral tree in its place. The legend claimed that the gleaming leaves and velvety red flowers are the symbols of her blood. The tree had replaced her body and now stood as a symbol of bravery and strength in the face of suffering.

Figure 9: Argentina's Coat of Arms

The coat of arms, from 1813, stands for truth and success. The red hat represents freedom and liberty. It originated from ancient Greece as a mark of free men. The rod holding up the hat was used in the ceremony of manumission, when slaves were formally emancipated. The laurel branches, again from Ancient Greece, stands for victory and glory. The national motto is: in unity there is power and in power there is freedom.

However, the truth is that these values were illusions for the Indian and Black peoples, as they were deliberately killed, erased, racialised and achievements forgotten from Argentina's national memory.

What are the main biomes in Argentina?

Temperate and humid biome: Buenos Ayres has a sunny temperate climate with four seasons. 'Pampa is a Quechua Indian word meaning "flat plain", according to *Encyclopaedia Britannica*, and surrounds Buenos Ayres. 'The Pampas … was wild country, severe, heroic, and flat as the ocean', according to writer, A. Lloyd (1951).

Figure 12: Gauchos on the Pampas

The Pampas is dry in the west, temperate in the east, and subtropical in the north, with not enough rain to grow a forest but enough to avoid a desert. Animals include guanacos and birds. The invaders tried to kill the Indians off the Pampas because it had rich fertile soil. Survivors were forced into reservations or prisons. Cattle were imported and large areas fenced off for Europeans who made immense fortunes in *estancias* and agriculture. Some *estancias* provide "authentic gaucho experiences", for tourists today.

Alpine Tundra Biome: The Aconcagua Mountain, the highest peak in the Western hemisphere at nearly 7000 metres high, is part of the Andes Mountain Range. The peak is a popular tourist destination for mountaineer climbers. It is snowy, windy and icy. Animals are llamas, alpacas and condors, that adapt by hibernating or have layers of fat and fur. Plants include lichens and mosses. Only the Indians who survived the invaders' oppression until the nineteenth century, lived in these areas.

Patagonia is cold and humid: One-third has sand dunes by the Atlantic Ocean; another third by the Andes mountains, with volcanoes and forests; another third has small, flat-topped mountains with a dry climate according to *Encyclopaedia Britannica*. Magellan penguins,

Figure 11: Regions in Argentina

dolphins, sea lions and elephant seals amongst others marine life are tourist attractions in the Valdés Península, a UNESCO Heritage site since 1999, in the Chubut province of Patagonia. Patagonia is the Spanish word for 'big foot' or 'giant'. The first colonists thought that the Indians were 'giants' and therefore this area was named Patagonia. Many Indians were exterminated or forced off this region, and then the Welsh people from the UK, immigrated and settled in, from 1865.

Figure 13: Mountains in the Alpine Tundra Biome

How are the natural features in danger?

Iguazú National Park: a spectacular waterfall in the shape of a horseshoe. Located in north-east Argentina, parts of Brazil and Paraguay. This waterfall '...is among the world's visually and acoustically most stunning natural sites...' according to UNESCO. Since 1984, it has been on the World Heritage List. The forest biome has about 2000 plant species, 80 tree species, 400 bird species and wild cat species although deforestation and pollution are causing difficulties.

Iguazú means 'Great Water' in Guarani language. The Guarani speakers claimed '... that their people had inhabited the forests... before the park was created.' They are '...demanding that a part of the park be declared as an Indian reservation', according to historian Dr Frederico Freitas. Although this claim is challenged.

Figure 14: Iguazu Falls on the border of Brazil and Argentina

The Gran Chaco: semi-arid and located in the north. Indian groups lived by hunting, gathering and fishing. Deliberate military attacks reduced their numbers. When the survivors were relocated to reservation areas, '...the Guarani speakers suffered all sorts of environmental problems: erosion by lake waters, contamination ... by pesticides ...', according to Dr Freitas.

The Chaco contains the second-largest forest, subtropical plants and the largest jaguar, *Panthera onca*, population which are in danger of extinction. Not only are the forests disappearing ... replaced with cattle *haciendas* and soya planting World Wildlife Organisation (WWF) but jaguars created a "landscape of fear", according to biologist Dr John Laundré.

Figure 15: Jaguars face threats, including hunting and habitat loss, and are now a protected species.

Iberá National Park: Located in the north-east Corrientes province. It is the second biggest wetlands in the world containing freshwater lagoons of swamps, floating islands and savannas. Despite the extermination of the jaguars in this region, the WWF has a 'rewilding project' to reintroduce them back into the environment, including giant anteaters and Pampas deer. Rural Corrientes people support the 'rewilding project' because '...jaguars are seen as powerful metaphors for their own independent and *guerrero* (warrior-like) culture', according to wildlife biologist Jessica Fort and her colleagues.

Chapter 1 Activities

Where is Argentina?
1. Locate, colour, and label Argentina, Chile, Peru, Brazil, and the United Kingdom on a world map. Name and label the oceans. Rank the countries in order of size at Nations Online https://www.nationsonline.org/oneworld/countries_byarea.htm
2. Watch this video - Continental Drift https://youtu.be/UvIDxu7twpc 1:32. Now compare with Plate tectonics.
3. What happened to some Africans when they landed in Río de la Plata? How many in total landed?
4. Alfred Wegener was a geologist. What is a geologist? https://www.geolsoc.org.uk/Geology-Career-Pathways/What-is-Geology/What-do-Geologists-do

What has silver got to do with it?
5. What does Rio de la Plata mean? What were the invaders looking for? Why?
6. How did America get its name? How did Buenos Aires get its name?
7. Use an atlas to locate Argentina. Then find it on a blank map to: a) colour in Buenos Ayres. b) label the Río de la Plata in the correct location.

How big is Argentina?
8. Learn countries of South America in this game. http://www.aaawhere.com/wo-map-capital-sa-ams.htm Which is the largest?
9. Thinking about the land area, which country is more crowded, UK or Argentina? Where would you like to live? Why/Why not?
10. Thinking about life expectancy and distance from the equator, which country would you prefer to live in? Why/Why not?

What are the national symbols of Argentina?
11. Think of your own symbol for each of these: a). Where you were born. b) What language you speak. c)What groups you belong to. d) What music/sport you like. e) What belief is important to you. f) 2 or 3 favourite colours. Then create your own identity flag using those symbols.
12. How do national customs relate to national identity?
13. Read the LEGEND. Do you believe this legend? Why/Why not? Create your own legend about one of Argentina's or UK's national symbols.

What are the main biomes in Argentina?
14. Watch Biomes of the World video https://youtu.be/P22epOXwJHg 2:07
15. Watch 7 Biomes of the World Facts video https://youtu.be/VExt_o7uM_c 17:08;
16. Watch this fascinating bird eye's view of the Argentina's regions. Called Argentina Desde El Aire. https://youtu.be/aKH_lqQnCzg 7:36
    Choose one biome that interests you the most and produce a double page fact sheet about it.

How are the natural features in danger?
17. Who or What is UNESCO? https://en.unesco.org/about-us/introducing-unesco
18. Read why jaguars are very important, WWF https://www.wwf.org.uk/learn/wildlife/jaguars and 10 Facts About Jaguars https://www.wwf.org.uk/learn/fascinating-facts/jaguars Then complete the quizzes. a) Watch the video about jaguar breeding in Iberá Park https://youtu.be/QfqZl4s3580 1:00

Chapter 2

Without Indians, there are no Americas	9
Who were the Patagonian Giants?	10
Who were Argentina's invaders?	11
In God and encomienda, we trust?	12
How did Indians avoid encomienda?	13
Were the Jesuit Missions an earthly paradise?	14
Chapter 2 Activities	15

Figure 16: Guarani speakers – one group of original peoples of Argentina.

Without Indians, there are no Americas

About 30,000 years ago, anthropologists believed that Patagonia was the first place in Argentina where people lived. They crossed the Bering Strait, when continents were connected to each other by huge ice sheets. Over thousands of years, experts said that they travelled south and spread over North America.

Thousands of years later, their great-grandchildren wandered south into South America, and then further down into Argentina. The first peoples to live in the Americas were the indigenous peoples, called Indians by the invaders. *'Sin indios no hay Indias'* was a popular sixteenth century phrase meaning, *'without Indians, there are no Americas'*.

Figure 17: Map showing the Bering Strait crossing from Russia to Alaska, Canada, into the Americas.

Argentinian Indians numbered over twenty different groups. A few are: Diaguitas in the North West who '...farmed terraced fields, ...built irrigation canals, ... kept herds of llama, ... produced elaborate ceramic industry. Metallurgy was also known', according to *Encyclopaedia Britannica*. Tupi-Guarani speakers lived in the North-East; Mapuche speakers inhabited the central area; and in the far south, were Tehuelches speakers. The Tupi–Guarani speakers numbered in the millions and were one of the largest ancient peoples. They were the ancient hunters and gatherers, fishers and farmers, and living for centuries in family villages.

'Guarani speakers consider themselves to belong to the same ethnic group and refer to each other as, "our kin", according to anthropologist Evaldo Mendes da Silva. They still migrate long distances in groups called 'wanderings'. Wanderings 'to celebrate weddings, parties, and religious rituals; to establish political alliances; to provide mutual assistance...', explained the anthropologist. However, today their 'wanderings' are disrupted due to modern border procedures and lack of paperwork.

The Mapuche speakers were the only Original peoples never conquered by the Spanish until the 19th century.

Mapuche speakers were known as warriors. About '113,680 lived in central Argentina', according to the *World Atlas*. They were farmers and lived with extended families. Evidence of their complex weaving techniques have been dated about 3300 years ago. At first, invaders stereotyped the Indians as 'noble, innocent, and primitive' meaning "at one with nature". They were then stereotyped as 'aggressive drunkards' or 'brutal, cannibalistic savages' to justify enslavement, elimination and appropriating the lands they lived on.

Who were the Patagonian Giants?

Tehuelche speakers were large groups of nomadic hunter and gatherer peoples living in Patagonia before the Spanish invaded. Patagonia was '...inhabited around eighth century by the possible ancestors of the first Tehuelche people of Patagonia', confirmed UNESCO.

UNESCO's archaeological investigations found cave paintings called *Cueva de las Manos* (Cave of Hands) as evidence of the Tehuelche people in this area between 13,000 and 9,500 years ago. These have survived untouched today and are visited by thousands of tourists.

In 1520, the Spanish invaders described the Tehuelche speakers as 'Giants' because they found huge footprints in the snow. This started the *Patagonian Giant myth.* Described as 'People, who in size come the nearest to giants of any people I believe in the world', and that they, 'wear as garments cloaks made of skins, well matched and sewn', wrote sixteenth century Spanish historian Pedro Sarmiento de Gamboa (1579-1580), 'making them look huge'.

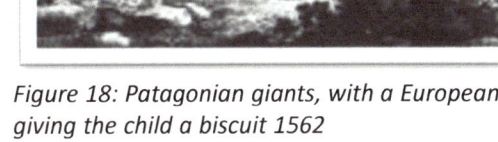

Figure 18: Patagonian giants, with a European giving the child a biscuit 1562

... so tall that our heads did not reach his leg (1536)

Eventually, delusion turned into reality when later explorers found the 'big foot' to be the guanaco-leather skin moccasins that made their footsteps look huge in the snow. The Patagonians wore animal skins as the climate further south nearer Antarctica, is very cold, and at times freezing. This made them appear larger than they were.

Figure 19: Cave of Hands, Santa Cruz Province

The Chubut province in Patagonia was the region where numerous Welsh people from the UK immigrated to, in 1865. This happened only after the 'Tehuelche speakers were defeated in a very lengthy and costly military campaign...' according to the *Cambridge Encyclopaedia*. That campaign was called the Conquest of the Desert, that deliberately killed thousands of Indian peoples to make way for European wealth, and power.

Who were Argentina's invaders?

In 1494, Portugal and Spain (Iberia) divided the world with an imaginary line between them, so that they would not interfere with each other's business; it was called the **Treaty of Tordesillas**.

Spain invaded countries to the left, whilst Portugal invaded countries to the right. From which, Europeans started their invasions, legalised the slave trade, enslavement and colonisation. The Treaty had no concern for the lives of people who already lived there.

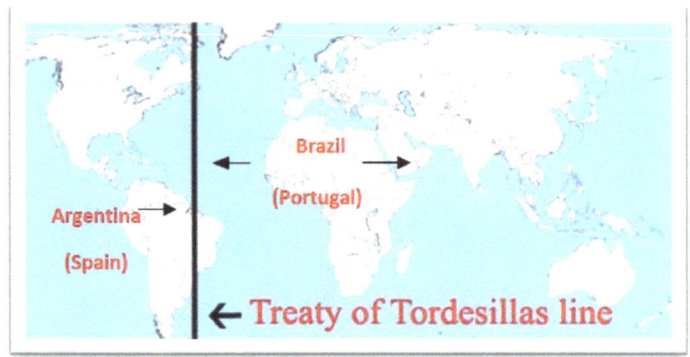

Figure 20: Spain gave up trading rights in Africa and Asia to Portugal

Amerigo Vespucci: born in Italy from a wealthy family and sailed for Iberia. In 1501-1502, he was searching for a new route to Asia. For Europeans, he recognised that where he had landed was not Asia but a 'new world'. The Americas were named after him.

Juan Díaz de Solís: born in Portugal and became the chief voyager for Spain after the death of Vespucci in 1512. He sailed for Spain in 1516 and thought the Río de la Plata was filled with silver. He was killed by local Guarani or Querandi speakers.

Ferdinand Magellan: born in Portugal but sailed for the Spanish royalty. Whilst avoiding the African coasts due to the Treaty of Tordesillas, he sailed through a passageway in the far south of Patagonia. It was named after him in 1519 as the Strait of Magellan.

Sebastian Cabot: born in Italy (or Bristol, in England), sailed for Spain and lived in England. In 1526, Cabot sailed to the Río de la Plata and found silver treasures in the river, giving the Río de la Plata its name.

Pedro de Mendoza: born into a 'distinguished Spanish family', and founder of the Buenos Ayres colony in 1536; this Spanish conquistador was driven out by Querandı speakers in 1537. He left wild horses which led to the rise of the roaming Pampas gauchos.

Juan de Garay: a Spanish conquistador. Buenos Ayres came under Spanish control again from 1580. Río de la Plata became the major slaving port. Cattle was imported that multiplied over the Pampas. Today, a monument where he first landed, stands in Plaza de Mayo.

John Strong: English captain, funded by Viscount of Falkland, first recorded landing on the islands in 1690. Due to the Treaty of Tordesillas, Spain fought wars with Britain over control. However, the Falklands Islands are now controlled by Britain since 1982.

In God and encomienda, we trust?

From 1503, Queen Isabella 1 of Spain gave Nicolas de Ovando, a Spanish governor, permission for priests and conquistadors to legally force Indians already living in the Río de la Plata region to work for them.

The Spanish Crown intended to stop the spread of Islam and convert the Indians to Catholicism. At the same time, exploit the land for gold and silver, to decorate their Iberian mansions and churches.

Encomienda meant granting areas of land to conquistadors who became Encomenderos. Encomenderos in charge demanded payments from the Indians already living there. Encomienda in English meant to entrust. Indian peoples should entrust the encomenderos to 'civilise them' through Catholic conversion; learning Spanish; digging for gold or silver; and protection from wars, including the Portuguese kidnappers from Brazil.

Figure 21: How the Indians Collect Gold from the Streams, 1528-98 by Jacques Le Moyne

Encomienda was the first racially-based enslavement

Repartimiento: Indian leaders had to provide their people, who were forced to work for a set number of days or months, to the encomenderos. They were forced to pay 'tributes', – an early form of 'protection money', according to the historians, – to the encomenderos for working on their own land. However, in return for 'entrusting' encomenderos, many Indians were slaughtered, enslaved, worked to death, sent in slavery back to Spain, or died from smallpox epidemics and other deadly European diseases.

The truth is that there was *'no trust'*. Encomienda turned into a cruel and brutal enslavement. Far away from Spain, corrupt encomienderos and middle-men abused the Indians for their own greed. Many ran away into the forests or died, and their numbers declined. Decreasing numbers of Indian labour led to replacement by African enslavement, mainly from West Central Africa. The Spanish Crown desired power and wealth, an empire, and now looked towards Africa for their labour needs.

How did Indians avoid encomienda?

Assimilation for some. This involved adopting Spanish appearance and culture. It seemed that appearance was extremely important to the Spanish. According to Spanish law, mixed-race descendants, a Spanish father and Indian mother, known as Mestizos, could not be forced into encomienda.

Figure 22: Mother and Daughter. The Tehuelche Indians of Patagonia.

Mestizo descendants then spoke Spanish, and adapted their traditions. Their skin colour became lighter as generations passed, until some became similar to *criollos* (locally born white Spanish descendants). So, the Indian enslaved population reduced substantially due to death, desertion, European diseases and assimilation.

... With my own eyes I saw Spaniards cut off the nose and ears of Indians, male and female, without provocation, merely because it pleased them to do it.
Quote 1: History of the Indies (1561) Bartolome de las Casas

Bartolomé de las Casas, a former encomendero, wrote eyewitness accounts about the abuses in the encomienda. Said to be a 'friend of the Indians', Bartolomé saw them as 'noble savages', as 'innocent sheep', or 'people devoid of craft, subtlety, and malice'. His writings called, *History of the Indies* and *Devastation of the Indies*, brought awareness to those in Spain, which may have led to the following legal changes:

It was upon these gentle lambs ... that ... the Spanish fell like ravening wolves upon the fold, or like tigers and savage lions who have not eaten meat for days.
Quote 2: Brief Account of the Devastation of the Indies 1522 Bartolomé de las Casas

The Burgos Law 1512-1513. Yet it was **The New Law of the Indies 1542** that freed Indians, and their future **enslavement was forbidden,** but the truth is, there was little enforcement. These laws were unpopular with the white *criollos* and encomenderos. Most had sunk so deeply into greed and cruelty that they fought and died against these laws. As a result, they carried on as before.

However, some Indians and their assimilated mixed-race descendants gradually left the encomienda, became rivals to Black labourers in the urban Buenos Ayres; or worked as peon wage labourers (debt bondage) on the Pampas countryside as gauchos or entered Jesuit Missions. The problem was, the Indian population declined rapidly, so the Spanish needed more enslaved labour.

Were the Jesuit Missions an earthly paradise?

Towns designed by Jesuit priests and built by Guarani speakers were called *Missions*. Built between 1610 and 1764, they were also known as *'Reducciones'*. The aim was to *reduce* the Indian and African peoples' culture by living with Jesuit missionaries. Jesuits would 'civilise' them and protect them from the encomienda. Today, four *Missions* are UNESCO World Heritage Sites and tourist attractions.

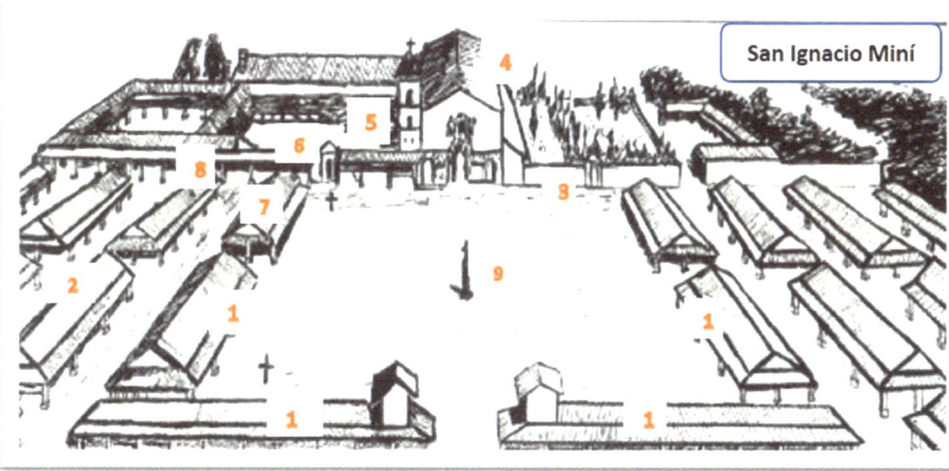

Figure 23: Match the numbers to the clues given in the activities. A general view of the Reducciones of San Ignacio Mini before its destruction. Junta Historica St Ignacio

In return, Indians replaced their hunting and gathering lifestyles with timetables, trading, Spanish language and religion. They produced agricultural goods and engaged in artisan activities for sale. An earthly paradise, as some Eurocentric historians believed. However, living in the *Missions* was not heaven on earth. They were exploited and maltreated, whilst the Jesuits preached Catholicism.

The War of the Seven Reducciones in 1756, changed the borders north of Río de la Plata. The Guarani speakers and Africans fought against the Europeans. Eventually, their resistance failed. This failure was used to discredit the Jesuits as traitors because Spain believed they became too wealthy and prevented the peoples from becoming 'fully civilised'. Therefore, 'King Charles III expelled 78 Jesuits in 1797, leaving about 89,000 Indians in the missions', according to historian Dr Julia Sarreal. Abandoned, the *Missions* then fell into decline.

Figure 24: San Ignacio Miní. One of the doors of the former church of the Jesuit-Guaraní mission

No more encomienda nor enslavement of the Indians led the Spanish Crown to dramatically increase the number of West Central Africans as the main labour source for the Río de La Plata region. The Spanish considered that '… the Negro …[was] worth as much as four Indians at work production…' wrote History Professor, Dr Ralph Vigil. However, the Treaty of Tordesillas prevented Spain from exporting directly from Africa. Whereas, Portugal had those rights, and were already involved in kidnapping people from the Kingdom of Kongo to their Brazilian colony.

Chapter 2 Activities

Without Indians, there are no Americas?
19. Locate Patagonia in an atlas. On a blank map, identify and colour in Patagonia.
20. Write a definition for the word 'stereotype'.
21. Write an essay as a Mapuche speaker in the year 1300, expressing your views on the arrival of the European invaders.

Who were the Patagonian Giants?
22. Why were Tehuelche speakers thought to be giants?
23. What message is Figure 18 trying to give? Is it fact or imagined? What did ordinary people in Europe think of this image?
24. Why did the Welsh people immigrate to Argentina in 1865. How did the Indians react to the arrival of the Welsh people?

Who were Argentina's invaders?
25. Did the conquistadors have the right to invade? Why/Why not? Why were they all men?
26. Research the monarchy in Iberia. Who were they and what did they do? How did they support the conquistadors?

In God and encomienda, we trust?
27. Explain what encomienda means. Watch Encomienda System by Shmoop https://youtu.be/BxMGtsGmwVg 2:22.
28. Give examples to show. a) What trust means. b) How trust is gained or broken? c) How trust can be 'repaired' if at all?
29. Draw a diagram in three parts to illustrate the encomienda system. Include intentions, what really happened, and the results.

How did Indians avoid Encomienda?
30. Why are primary sources important? How many on this page?
31. Watch more information about Bartolomé de las Casas https://youtu.be/1XmuQvvqsZU 6:57.
32. Look at the Figure 22. What might the mother and daughter have been thinking about, before during and after the photo.

Were the Jesuit Missions an earthly paradise?
33. Look closely at the layout plan of the San Ignacio Mini Jesuit Mission. Match the numbers on the plan to these room clues:
    1. where people live/sleep
    2. where people in charge meet and set rules
    3. where dead people live
    4. where believers pray together
    5. where people learn in groups
    6. where people eat together in groups
    7. where people prepare food to eat
    8. where people make things to sell and trade
    9. an ancient way to tell the time

Chapter 3

What is the legacy of the Kongo Kingdom?	17
Why was the Kongo Princess burned at the stake?	18
Could diamonds be forever?	19
What was the Assiento de Negroes?	20
To raid or not to raid; is that the question?	21
What is the fallacy of Africans selling each other?	22
What is the fallacy of Africans selling each other 2?	23
Floating tombs, – a way to die?	24
What is the evidence of chattel enslavement?	25
Chattel enslavement activities	26
How many were raced across the Atlantic?	27
Who was sold to the highest bidder?	28
Chapter 3 Activities	29-30

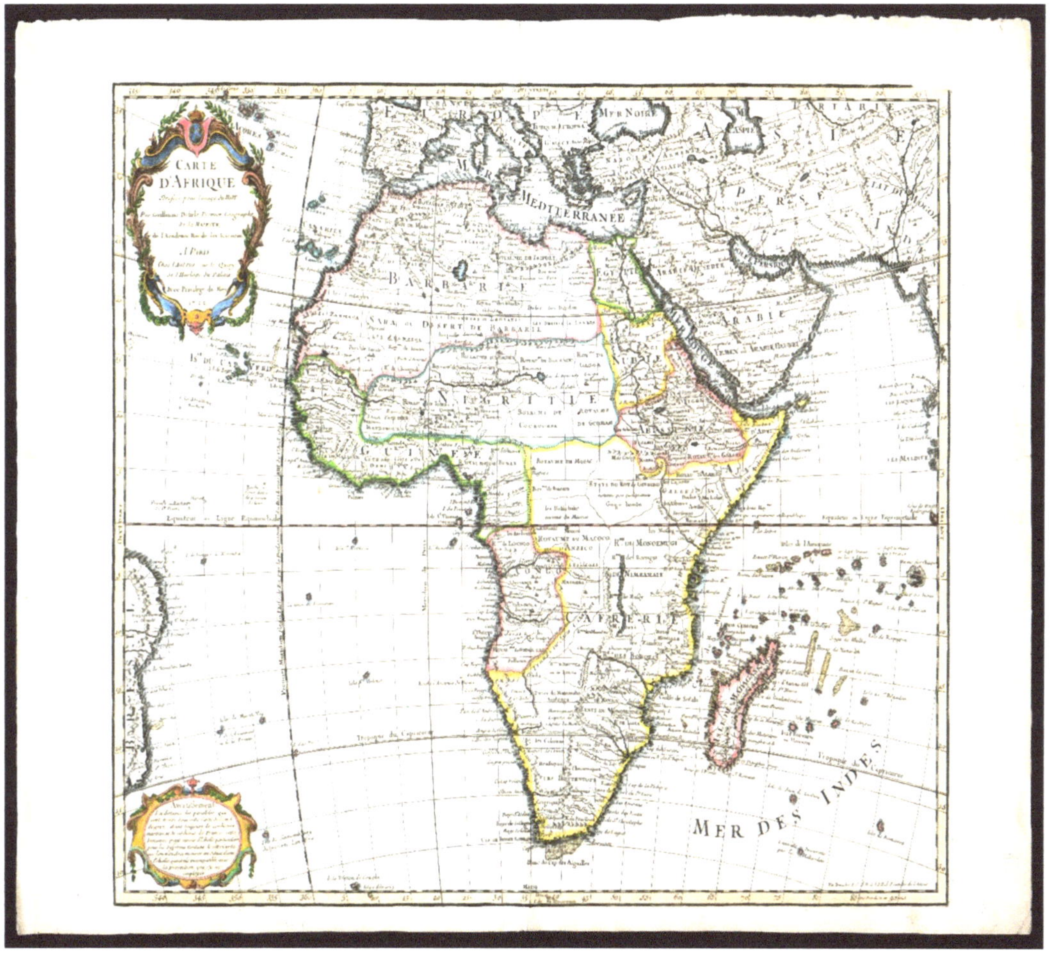

Figure 25: Carte d'Afrique by Guillaume Delisle 1745 The kingdom of Kongo from 14-19th century CE. It was the Portuguese, who changed the spelling of Kongo to a 'C' s in Congo today. The Kingdom of Kongo in West Central Africa covered an area larger than England, UK at 150,000 km^2 approx. versus 130,395 km^2 approx.

What is the legacy of the Kongo Kingdom?

Kongo is Angola today, parts of the Democratic Republic of Congo, the Republic of Congo, and Gabon. 'Angola comes from the word Ngola which was an iron object that symbolised kingship', wrote Dr Joseph C. Miller. 'Over two million people lived in a highly organised civilisation called the Kingdom of Kongo by the 1400s. Much like Europe at that time', confirmed Dr Christine Saidi.

Manikongo Afonso 1 (1456-1542) was the greatest and sixth King of the Kongo from the Kilukeni lineage until 1543. He had absolute power and friendly trading with Portugal. 'They exchanged copper, ivory, 'beautiful' and 'peerless' raffia-palm cloth', and 'some slaves in small quantity', said Portuguese explorer Duarte Pacheco Pereira in 1506, 'for European products'. Historians believed that his son, Henrique, became the first Black Bishop in the Catholic Church in 1518.

Eurocentric historians thought that the Kongolese 'converted wholeheartedly' to Catholicism. Yet, the truth is that the Kongolese linked their cosmology beliefs and ancestor worship together with Catholicism. 'They [the Kongolese] simply created space in their physical and spiritual worlds for Catholic Christianity', according to University History Professor Ras Michael Brown.

This friendly trade enriched the Kingdom but also weakened it. The Portuguese found that enslaving people made them the most money. Instead of trading war captives and criminals, freeborn citizens were kidnapped as well. Using divide and conquer tactics, guns and firearms, the Portuguese incited rebellions, bribed leaders and made allies with rival states, incited civil wars to produce even more war captives. By 1526, King Afonso could not stop the corrupt Portuguese. He wrote letters of complaint (Quote 3).

Figure 26. King of Kongo on a throne surrounded by Dutch bodyguards. The Dutch had captured Luanda from the Portuguese in 1641 but they were defeated in 1648.

> King Afonso wrote long letters of complaint to kings Manuel I and João III of Portugal ...
>
> ...*merchants daily seize our subjects... Thieves and men of evil conscience take them because they wish to possess the things and wares of this Kingdom... They grab them and cause them to be sold; and so great, Sir, is their corruption and licentious-ness that our country is being utterly depopulated...* Quote 3: Letters to the King of Portugal 1526 October 18, 1526

After the Jaga (Portuguese named) attacks from 1569, plus the artificial geographical boundaries created by the Portuguese, that displaced many people; **'the European slavery trade was a key factor in the destablisation and wars ... [which] eventually led to a decline of the Kongo Kingdom'**, said African Professor, Dr Fikru Gebrekidan. But ' ... just as in Europe, Asia, and the Americas, large and powerful kingdoms in Africa did not last forever', said historian Dr Saidi. Today, King Afonso 1 is seen as too innocent and trusting to understand European dishonesty, or a great resistance figure who opposed European domination and slavery.

Why was the Kongo Princess burned at the stake?

Kimpa Vita Nsimba, baptised Dona Beatriz Kimpa Vita was a revolutionary prophetess of the Antonian Movement. In typical European medieval custom, she was burned at the stake with her child, in 1706 for "witchcraft" and "heresy". Born in 1684, from Kongo royalty with military backgrounds, Kimpa grew up during the civil wars which created captives for the European slave trade. Mbanza Kongo (São Salvador in Portuguese), was the capital city where former kings were buried. Abandoned in 1678, Mbanza Kongo is now a World Heritage Site since 2017.

Kimpa Vita had 'visions' during childhood. Later, she became a *Nganga Marinda,* a messenger for the spirits. Upon recovery from a near death experience, she became Saint Anthony of Padua. He was an important patron saint of lost souls, mothers and children, the poor, performed miracles and preached peace. As a teenager, Kimpa taught that St Anthony was a Black African who wanted her to stop the civil wars; stop the Portuguese slave trade, rebuild and repopulate Mbanza Kongo. Historians said that she 'healed people, and cured the infertile.'

According to Dr Aurelien Gampiot, Sociologist of Religion, in 'Kimpa Vita's eyes, the Kingdom of Kongo was the real holy land', and '… belonged to the Black race'. Kimpa rejected '… the biblical myth of the curse of Ham, ' and argued that 'Jesus and the Madonna were Kongolese and Black'. She insisted that 'Mbanza Kongo was Bethlehem, and heaven was for Africans, not just whites [only]'. 'Kimpa Vita's extolling Blackness went hand in hand with a rejection of whiteness, which was connected to evil', wrote Dr Gampiot.

Figure 27: By Bernardo da Gallo. A representation of Kimpa Vita

Priest Barnardo da Gallo, was furious when thousands abandoned white Catholicism for the Anthonian Movement. Kimpa believed the 'Capuchins [monks] were corrupt, cruel and teaching a false Christianity', with their involvement in the slave trade, contradictory to Christian doctrine.

> Bernardo da Gallo described the disconcerting sight of **"that woman"** *gliding "on tiptoes," her hips and body slithering "like a snake," while she carried her head straight and" her neck stretched." She appeared to be floating above the ground rather than walking…*
> Quote 4, Cecile Fromont, (2014-11-24). Art of Conversion: Christian Visual Culture in the Kingdom of Kongo.

The truth is that Kimpa Vita practised non-violent resistance, against European domination; preached unity and Black nationalism. She also proved that a woman could be a male reincarnate. Her followers, continued her messages after her death. Some historians believe that, followers who were later enslaved, carried out revolts such as the USA Stono Rebellion, the Haiti Revolution and the Maroon Wars in Jamaica.

Could diamonds be forever?

Figure 28: The skyline of Luanda-Capital city of Angola is Luanda

Angola became a Portuguese colony. The capital, Luanda was founded in 1587, and Benguela from 1617. Enslavement within Angola was abolished in 1875 though the slave-owning Portuguese settlers, exploited Angolan labour until early twentieth century. Independence took place in 1975. Today, Luanda is modern and bustling, but most people live in unmodernised rural areas. Portuguese is the official language, with Bantu-speaking Angolans.

Aquaculture: According to Food and Agriculture Organisation of the United Nations in 2020, 'Fish plays an important role in the Angolan diet.' And '70% of Angolans are employed in the fishing industry.' With a coastline of about 1,650 km in length, and rich fishing grounds, this is the third most important sector for the Angolan economy.

Figure 29: Fish market: Provincial market on Cahama-Chibia-Lubango road (Huila Province, Angola).

Diamonds: 'Angola has the potential to become the largest diamond mining country in the world', reported Mining Review. US$1.5 billion worth of diamonds are produced every year. But between 1961 and 2002, **'conflict'** or **'blood' diamonds**, funded civil wars immediately after independence. Thousands of Angolans died. Today, the United Nations Kimberley Process ensures human rights.

Oil is a natural resource. 'Angola has become one of the largest exporters of petroleum in … Africa', according to *Encyclopaedia Britannica*. Some say it is 'the Kuwait of Africa'. From involvement in the European slave trade to colonisation and civil wars, Angolan growth today, includes diamonds, oil, and aquaculture.

The truth is, profits from oil, diamonds and fisheries filters down to ordinary Angolans instead of European countries. Many lack basic necessities outside of the capital since Angolan enslavement and the damage and disruption of the slave trade. Once independence was gained, civil wars followed financed by 'blood diamonds'. However, before the Portuguese invaders, the **Kingdom of Kongo was a great ancient civilisation.**

What was the Assiento de Negroes?

In 1493, the Pope gave permission, called papal bulls, for Iberia (Spain and Portugal) to enslave those who do not practise Catholicism. The Spanish Crown and the Catholic Church agreed with the slave trade. Due to the 1494 Treaty of Tordesillas, Spain had no direct presence in Angola. So issued licences to individuals but the captives were sent infrequently.

By 1713, Spain provided royal contracts called **Assiento de Negroes** for advanced payment and specified numbers to buy and sell Angolans into Río de la Plata. Banks such as Barclays and the Bank of England were set up to fund slaving vessels, loans, credits and insurances; funds for factories to make guns, gunpowder, shackles, clothes and shoes. By the nineteenth century, Britain became known as 'Great' Britain because it became the largest slaving nation.

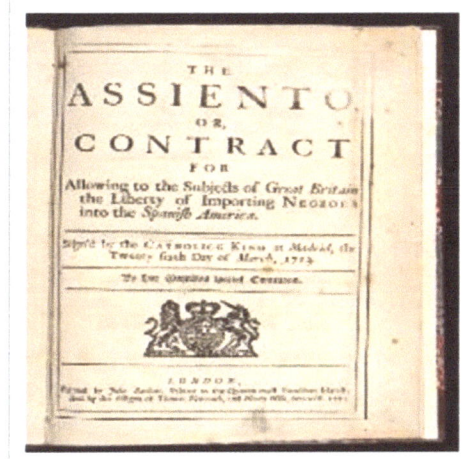

Figure 30: The Assiento de Negroes, 1713

London, Liverpool, Bristol ... became extremely wealthy from slavery profits, funding part of the Industrial Revolution

French Guinea Company: In 1635, France was the third largest slavers that paid for *L'Assiento*. 40,000 enslaved were brought to the Retiro slave market in Río de la Plata between 1703-1713.

British South Sea Company: Under the Treaty of Utrecht, Britain supplied Spain with 'negroes' from 1713. Britain paid the Spanish Crown for a thirty-year *Assiento de Negroes*. About 75,000 were enslaved.

Royal Company of the Philippines: Spain shipped 2,900 Africans between 1788-1789. British vessels used this company as well, to transport enslaved directly from Portuguese 'factories' in Angola.

The **Portuguese** and the **United States** had *Assientos* into Río de la Plata, using British or French vessels. Also, the Dutch had 20% of the trade to Spanish Americas between 1658 and 1729.

In 1776, Viceroyalty of the Río de la Plata was formed, but Spain's frequent wars with other European nations disrupted their slaving missions. Thus, Spain started free trade, which meant no more *Assientos*. This led to smuggling and piracy. The exact number of people who entered Río de la Plata after 1776 is unknown, because corrupt officials did not keep records.

To raid or not to raid; is that the question?

Now that Europeans had 'royal and godly permissions' to invade Angola, they went with force, violence and dishonest trades. One of those trades was in firearms. According to Economic Historian Warren Whatley, Britain was exporting between 100,000 and 200,000 muskets into West Africa by the eighteenth century. In fact, in 1730, evidence from the Dutch Director-General Elmina dungeons, along the coast of West Africa said: (Quote 5)

Figure 31: Late 18th century flintlock blunderbuss gun is on display at International Slavery Museum. Accession number 60.86.1

The truth is, the 'trade' in guns were of poorer quality than European firearms. Europeans engaged in trickery, local kidnappings, small-scale violence, exchanging criminals, those held as pawns for unpaid debts and war captives for guns, iron weapons and gunpowder. Luso African descendants (Portuguese fathers and African mothers) acted as collaborators who encouraged conflict, disputes and arguments. As the guns-for-slaves-cycle increased (Figure 31), African regions became underdeveloped and depopulated over four centuries. The increasing rate of capture due to gun violence meant to raid or be raided instead.

Escaping the slave trade meant hiding in, '...caverns, caves, and cliff walls...' where '...the ability to watch the lowlands and incoming paths ... afforded protection', according to Economics Professor Nathan Nunn. For that reason, 'rugged terrain was a positive advantage', and disrupted the Portuguese slave raiders. Yet, escaping raids resulted in mass refugees leading to mixed ethnicities, languages, loss of kinship lineages and less permanent dwellings.

> *The great quantity of guns ... Europeans have brought ... caused terrible wars between the Kings ..., who made their prisoners of war slaves; these slaves were immediately brought up by Europeans at steadily increasing prices ... to renew their hostilities... using all sorts of pretexts to attack each other or reviving old disputes.* Quote 5: Dutch Director General at Elmina No. 596 Short Memoir, 1730

Eurocentric historians forget that Africa is a vast and immense continent with '...more than 2000 distinct ethnic groups and languages ...' proven by 'mitochondrial DNA (mtDNA)', according to geneticists Dr Sarah Tishkoff and others. Such diversity may mean that they have no more affinity to different groups than the European warring nations did to each other. The truth is, '... attacks on neighbouring states led to a culture of mistrust ... [that] persists to this day', said Professor Nunn. Rather than collaborate and trade peacefully, as some Eurocentric historians have written in their history books, most African rulers were forced to deliver and sell people at gunpoint. History Professor Dr Herbert Foster said that, 'African states took up slave raiding in self-protection since guns could be only bought with slaves'. A vicious cycle started by the Europeans!

What is the fallacy of Africans selling each other?

Shifting the guilt and blaming Africans for the European slave trade. The truth is that:
1. The white Eurocentric meaning of "slave" was different to the African meaning of "slave".
2. Africans did not see themselves as "Africans" but belonging to "kingdoms or kinship groups".
3. An example of this distorted fallacy, African Professor Dr Molefi Asante said, '**Blacks were police officers in ... South Africa but one cannot blame apartheid on Black people.**'
4. An enslaved in African countries was in servitude, a servant. 'Who not only had rights, but often became vassals, vassals often became free men, and free men sometimes became chiefs', wrote Professor Herbert Forster. African "slavery" was colourless and similar to feudal Europe. Based on land ownership, rulers were at the top, with peasants at the bottom.

Figure 32: Primary source from the British Library. The Interesting Narrative of the Life of Olaudah Equiano. 1789.

Olaudah Equiano, confirmed this when he was kidnapped as a child and described his experience (Quote 6). African captives then, were usually outsiders, homeless, criminals or war captives. Also, Professors of Economic Historians Dr James Fenske and others said that, 'Crises... pushed people to sell themselves or their dependants ...'. The Little Ice Age in the seventeenth century led to droughts and famines causing such crises. Then again, demand can reduce due to increased 'deaths and dispersion', thus increasing slave raiding for even more captives.

Chattel comes from the word 'cattle'

'*...they were only prisoners of war, or such among us as had been convicted of kidnapping, or adultery, and some other crimes, which we esteemed heinous...*'
Quote 6: The interesting life of Olaudah Equiano 1789

Evidence proved that Europeans created chattel slavery. It meant owning a human person like a pet. It was the law; became associated with skin colour and passed down the generations. Europeans invented racism against African people to justify enslavement for their own wealth and power. Europeans had the *assientos*, approved by royalty and the church; invaded the West African coast and interior with guns, some poor quality goods, deceit trickery and bribes, created the middle passage, enslavement and colonisation, **not the other way around**.

Since the fifteenth century, trading was used, '...as a cover beneath which violent raiding, kidnapping and wars operated', confirmed African Professor Dr Ntloedibe. Dr Ntloedibe highlighted that a few 'greedy and despotic rulers ... enticed by European goods to kidnap and sell their own people into slavery', does not mean that it was fair or an equal partnership between the European invaders and the 'greedy and despotic rulers'. Therefore, the truth is that the guilt of the European slave trade lies firmly with the Europeans.

What is the fallacy of Africans selling each other 2?

Eurocentric historians believe that their ancestors:
- 'did not raid or kidnap or steal Africans', and were 'invited to Africa by African rulers'
- 'transatlantic slave trade lasted so long due to the African chiefs',
- 'simply tapped into the existing market', and 'did not go into the interior'

> *I was resident for seven months at a factory in Mossula Bay, in the kingdom of Angola. I know of no other way of making slaves there, than by robbery … They were always armed when they went out. They took no goods with them, but yet returned with slaves.* Quote 7: British abolitionist, Thomas Clarkson 1787

These are gross distortions. Kongolese people were not simply '**sitting on the beach by millions**!' insisted Walter Rodney, a Guyanese historian, waiting for Europeans to load them onto their slaving vessels! Yet, the Eurocentric historians agreed that snatching people started in the early fifteenth century but then, for whatever reason, they said it stopped. It was just a few rogue ship captains that continued to seize Kongolese people! However, a quote from British abolitionist Thomas Clarkson in 1787 said otherwise. Slavers pretended to trade in the daytime; returned at night to kidnap people using the information already gathered whilst day trading!

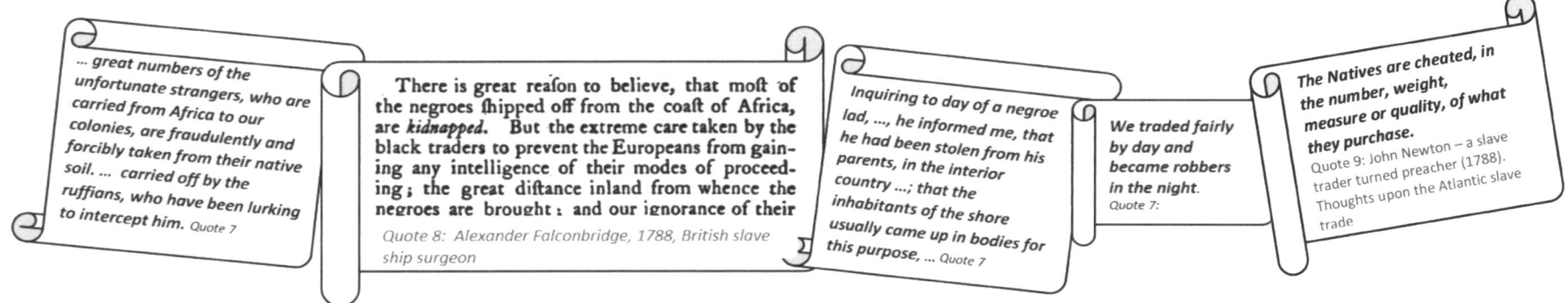

> *… great numbers of the unfortunate strangers, who are carried from Africa to our colonies, are fraudulently and forcibly taken from their native soil. … carried off by the ruffians, who have been lurking to intercept him.* Quote 7

> *There is great reason to believe, that most of the negroes shipped off from the coast of Africa, are kidnapped. But the extreme care taken by the black traders to prevent the Europeans from gaining any intelligence of their modes of proceeding; the great distance inland from whence the negroes are brought: and our ignorance of their* Quote 8: Alexander Falconbridge, 1788, British slave ship surgeon

> *Inquiring to day of a negroe lad, …, he informed me, that he had been stolen from his parents, in the interior country …; that the inhabitants of the shore usually came up in bodies for this purpose, …* Quote 7

> *We traded fairly by day and became robbers in the night.* Quote 7:

> *The Natives are cheated, in the number, weight, measure or quality, of what they purchase.* Quote 9: John Newton – a slave trader turned preacher (1788). Thoughts upon the Atlantic slave trade

The truth is that, 'There were more than three thousand episodes of slave flights in Luanda and nearby regions between 1846 and 1876', argued Dr. José Curto; aided and abetted by other African rulers and ordinary people. Rather than Africans sold Africans, people had to flee from their homes. This led to maroon communities numbering in the thousands called mutolos or quilombos. More people might have been captured if the mutolos or quilombos had not severely disrupted the Portuguese slavers' networks.

Remember that the Europeans invaded, created the middle passage; took advantage of environmental and climatic crises and used force and deceit to gain more captives. Those greedy enough to be tricked increased the rate of capture. It was the Portuguese that colonised Angola (Kongo); started kidnapping and raiding; used control and divide tactics aided by guns and gunpowder. They used their mixed-raced (mulattoes) descendants as go-betweens, slave and raid catchers. **Not the other way around.**

Floating tombs – a way to die?

With or without Assientos, slavers kidnapped, forced millions onboard slaving ships to cross the Atlantic Ocean, called the Middle Passage, and sold West Central African people to the Americas between 1500s and 1900s. This was not the same as other peoples who immigrated to the 'New World' to work as 'indentured servants'. Eurocentric historians, who believed that the African enslaved were the same as indentured servants, attempt to distort the truth. **There has been nothing before it or after it, in the history of mass-scale legal deportation of peoples from one continent to another.**

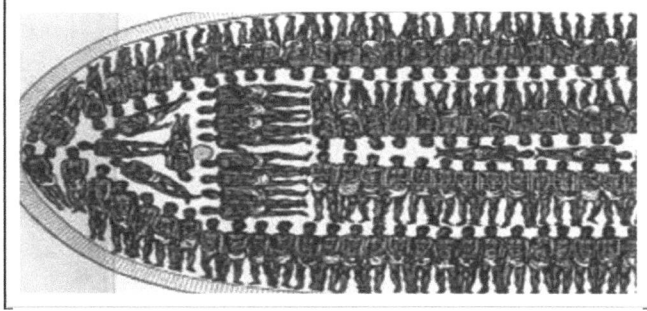

Figure 33: British (built in Liverpool) Brookes slave ship, 1780s and named after its owner and builder, James Brooks.

> *The opinion that the number of slaves were said to be crowded in them is groundless [untrue]. On the voyage from Africa to the West Indies, the Negroes are well fed, comfortable and have every attention paid to their health, cleanliness and convenience. When upon deck they amused themselves with dancing. In short, the voyage from Africa to the West Indies was one of the happiest periods of a negro's life.'*
>
> QUOTE 10: From A Short Account of the African Slave Trade by Robert Norris. Liverpool Museum. What image is Robert Norris attempting to show in this report?

> **6 June 1770:** "The slaves made an insurrection [rebellion] which was soon quelled [stopped] with the loss of two women."
>
> **23 June 1770:** "Died a girl slave, No. 13. The slaves attempted an insurrection, lost a man who jumped over board and was drown'd. Employed securing the men in chains and gave the women concerned 24 lashes each."
>
> **26 June 1770:** "The slaves this day proposed making an insurrection and a few of them got off their handcuffs but were detected [seen] in time."
>
> **27 June 1770:** "The slaves attempted to escape from the hold in the night with a design to murder the whites or drown themselves, but were stopped by the watch. In the morning they confessed their intention and the women as well as the men were determined to jump overboard but in case of being prevented by their irons were resolved as their last resource to burn the ship. Their obstinacy (actions) put me under the necessity of shooting the leader." irons were resolved as their last resource to burn the ship. Their obstinacy (actions) put me under the necessity of shooting the leader." Ship'
>
> QUOTE 11: Ship's log recorded by Captain Robert Norris of the Liverpool slave ship. Liverpool Museum

Slaving vessels included the Brookes, to steam-powered and clipper ships, that 'raced' along the Atlantic Ocean resulting **in 'one huge graveyard and a crime scene',** declared actor Samuel L Jackson in the BBC series Enslaved 2020. The Angolan captured were imprisoned in barracoons, – infested warehouses on the coast before being loaded onto slaving vessels.

To prevent mutinies, different cultures and languages were thrown together. Despite the shackles, guns and whips, many Africans resisted and were successful survivors. Some Luso Africans served as interpreters, sailors or 'guardians'.

Living conditions were inhuman and unsanitary. There was little food, and the stench could not be described. Experts say that more than 1.5 million African peoples died from diseases or drowning. The truth is that African spirit and cultural traits did not simply drift away on these floating prison ships, but with the strength of the human spirit, **over 12 million survived**.

What is the evidence of chattel enslavement?

How do we know how the enslaved were treated?

Look at this document carefully. It is a sales account record; some call it or similar accounts, "the book of the dead". It records the selling of goods and captives.

Answer the activities in the black box on the next page and then in the red box to find evidence of how people were treated.

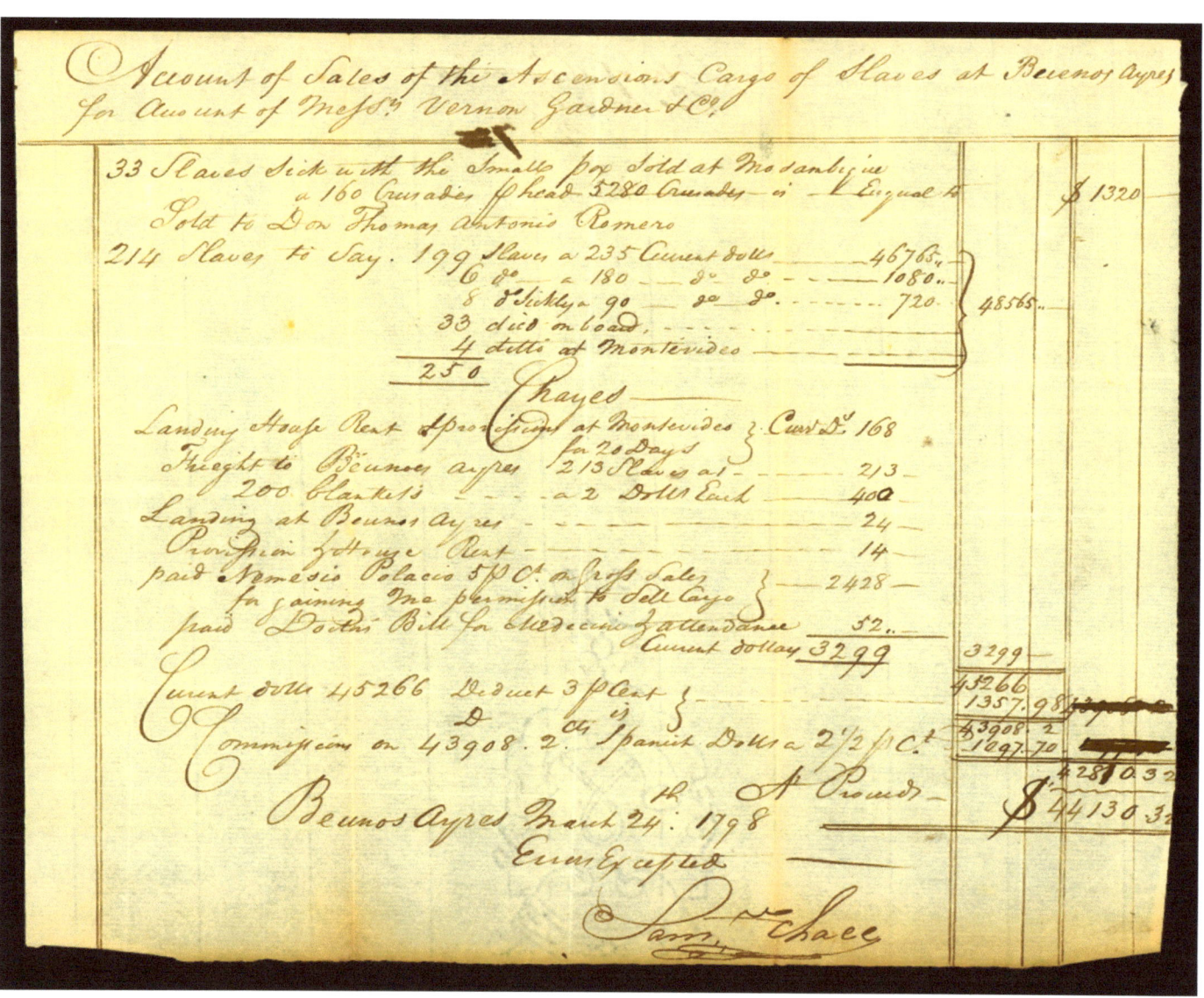

Figure 34: Account of Sales of the Ascensions Cargo of Slaves and Buenos Ayres for Account of Messrs. Vernon Gardner & Co. March 24, 1798. Slavery Collection, Series 1: Samuel and William Vernon, Subseries 2: Business Papers. New-York Historical Society Library

Chattel enslavement activities

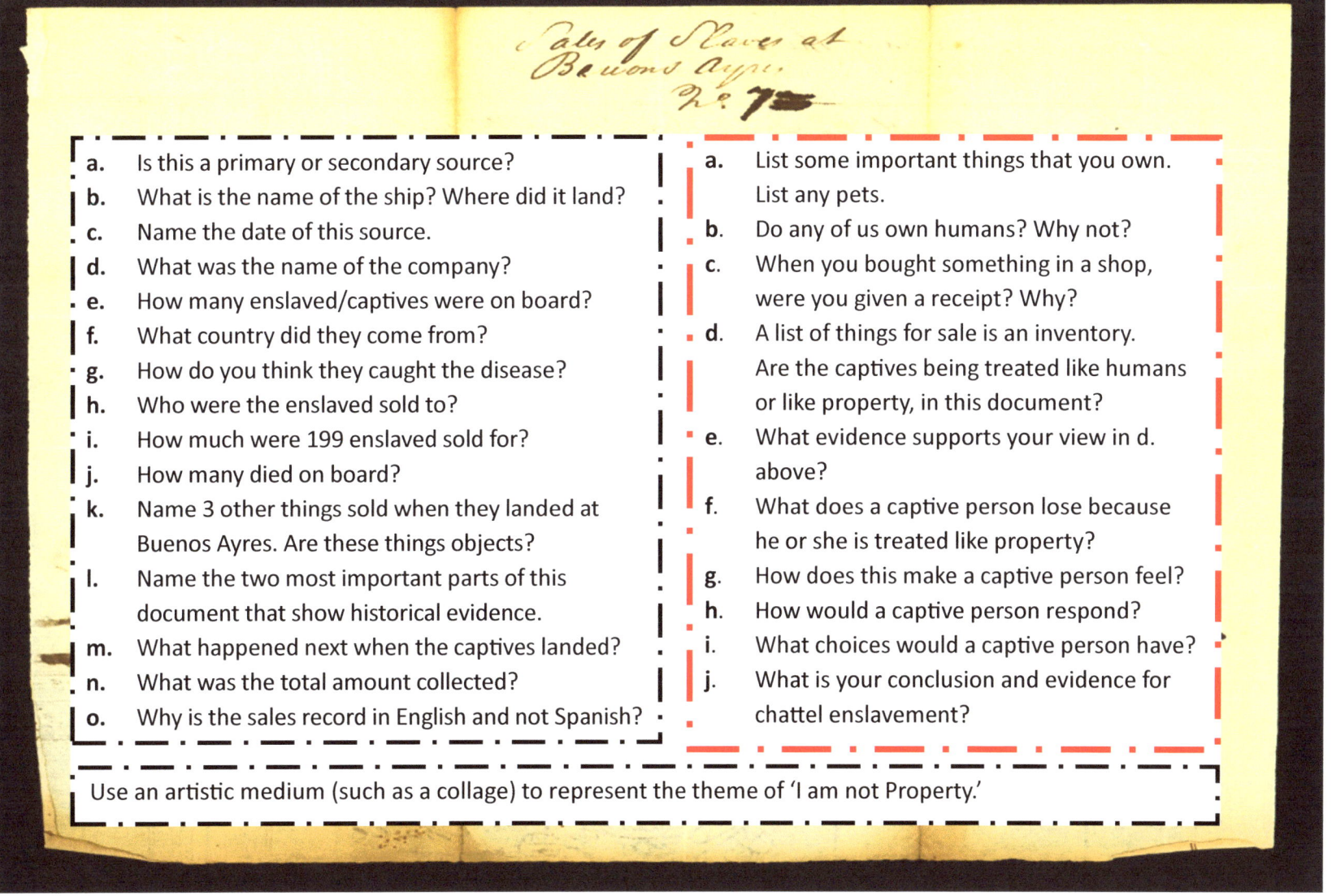

a. Is this a primary or secondary source?
b. What is the name of the ship? Where did it land?
c. Name the date of this source.
d. What was the name of the company?
e. How many enslaved/captives were on board?
f. What country did they come from?
g. How do you think they caught the disease?
h. Who were the enslaved sold to?
i. How much were 199 enslaved sold for?
j. How many died on board?
k. Name 3 other things sold when they landed at Buenos Ayres. Are these things objects?
l. Name the two most important parts of this document that show historical evidence.
m. What happened next when the captives landed?
n. What was the total amount collected?
o. Why is the sales record in English and not Spanish?

a. List some important things that you own. List any pets.
b. Do any of us own humans? Why not?
c. When you bought something in a shop, were you given a receipt? Why?
d. A list of things for sale is an inventory. Are the captives being treated like humans or like property, in this document?
e. What evidence supports your view in d. above?
f. What does a captive person lose because he or she is treated like property?
g. How does this make a captive person feel?
h. How would a captive person respond?
i. What choices would a captive person have?
j. What is your conclusion and evidence for chattel enslavement?

Use an artistic medium (such as a collage) to represent the theme of 'I am not Property.'

Figure 35: Page 2. Account of Sales of the Ascensions Cargo of Slaves and Buenos Ayres for Account of Messrs. Vernon Gardner & Co. March 24, 1798. Slavery Collection, Series 1: Samuel and William Vernon, Subseries 2: Business Papers. New-York Historical Society Library.

How many were raced across the Atlantic?

Buenos Ayres is now the "Paris of South America". 'The population ... is estimated at one hundred thousand inhabitants, including Whites, Negroes, Mestizoes, and Indians', said British explorer, Samuel Haigh, 1817. New flashy buildings, houses, streets, plazas, were built to resemble Europe, now a major area of international trade.

Between 1695 and 1850, Benguela sent nearly half a million enslaved to the 'new world'. Except Luso Africans who were mulattoes. 'Portuguese agents … avoided enslaving mulattoes in West Central Africa, since mulattoes were descendants of whites, who by definition, were free people', wrote University Professor Mariana Candido. Instead, they remained in Angola to be used as slave and raid catchers.

Figure 36: Foreign conquest, as drawn by Europeans

Dr Alex Borucki calculated a total of **70,225** enslaved were imported between 1777 and 1812. His research of the Spanish records, port and ship logs confirmed that most of the enslaved came directly from Brazil to Río de la Plata rather than across the Atlantic from West Central Africa, making journeys more hazardous. He stated that **'…** the Río de la Plata was still reliant on Brazil for its slaves', carried '…by the Royal Company of the Philippines'.

African American anthropologist Irene Digg's 1742 research found that, **12,473** enslaved came to Buenos Ayres from Brazil. So, about one-quarter that left Angola and ended up in Río de la Plata, called in at another port before landing in Buenos Ayres; **136,100** were shipped from Brazil's Río de Janeiro port according to Slave Voyages.org.

The truth is, Dr Kara Schultz calculated Intra-American routes (Figure 37), in addition to the crossings on the Atlantic Ocean. Furthermore, DNA genetic studies of 391 samples by Dr Marina Muzzio and others found, '… a large proportion of the ships …came from Mozambique…' as well as Loango and Angola. Jamaica, Barbados, and Cuba also formed more Intra-American routes, with much smaller numbers into Río de la Plata. However, what ever numbers are known, the totality does not include the widespread smuggling and piracy once the Spanish Crown opened up to free trade.

First Known Port of Origin	Number of Vessels (% of total)	Known captives disembarked
Rio de Janeiro	71 (53)	4775
Bahia	28 (21)	1738
Pernambuco	11 (8)	671
São Vicente/Santos	4 (3)	141
Brazil, port not specified	20 (15)	968
TOTAL	133	8283

Figure 37: Origin of 133 intra-American slaving vessels arriving in the port of Buenos Ayres, 1586-1680 by Dr. Kara D Schultz:

Who was sold to the highest bidder?

Some historians believed that it was mainly young Kongolese males in the earliest centuries. Certainly, after British abolition of 1807 and the 1830s, 'children made up to 40% and women a further 15%', according to African American Professor of History, Maghan Keita. Once at Buenos Ayres, however, the African born or *bozales* who did not speak Spanish were taken to filthy slave markets for auction at:

Parque Lezama: owned by the French Guinea Company, then the Lezama family who sold it to the city. Now a renowned park and location of the National Museum of History in San Telmo, a former enslaved *barrio* of Buenos Ayres.

El Retiro: owned by the British South Sea Company; underground cellars and factories, near Plaza San Martin in the *barrio* of San Telmo. Now a private museum.

Old Customs House: near the river, owned by the Azcuenaga family on Balcarce and Belgrano Streets or Basavilbaso House, who paid to keep their enslaved there. Now the Casa Rosada museum.

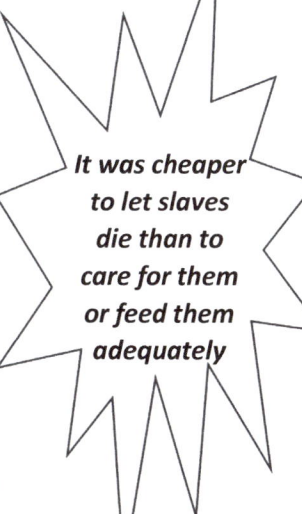

Figure 38: Black for sale without defects, "Diario de la Marina", published on February 3, 1846 from Spanish Newspaper-ABC History

> *the wind that generally prevails, is most harmful to the health of the public [...] because as the negroes tend to arrive with illnesses, full of scabies and scurvy and issuing from their body a fetid and pestilent odor, they may through their proximity infect the city.*
> Quote 12: Excerpt from Maxine Hanon. (2001) in Daniel Schavelzon (2014): On Slaves and Beer.

Auctions took place in 'El Retiro ... on an ample platform, like a stage', highlighted University Professor Daniel Schavelzon, 'priced according to size, strength and potential'. Punishments included 'whips and stocks'. He said they were inspected for weight and height measurements, after which they were set a price. 'Before being sold, they were washed and cleaned, and fats and oils were rubbed into their skin'. He continued that, 'Hot tar was rubbed into any sores or wounds, and they were dressed in rags. This was called 'seasoning'.

Sick Africans were labelled as waste, sold cheaply, or left to perish on the docks as Professor Schavelzon pointed out. Others were branded like cattle, named after the owner, chained in lines, or loaded onto carts and taken far into the interior to other provinces, or bought as domestics, silver or gold mine labourers. Black captives were specifically directed to be agriculturalists and labourers on *estancias* (large cattle farms) according to the experts.

It was cheaper to let slaves die than to care for them or feed them adequately

Chapter 3 Activities

What is the legacy of the Kongo Kingdom?
34. Watch the City of Mbanza Kongo Africa's Great Civilizations https://youtu.be/nGTNJ1S0TU0 2:43. Watch HomeTeam History – A History of the Bakongo People https://youtu.be/YnICBj18SX0 9:16
35. Does it appear that King Afonso I was opposed to all slave trading, or only certain kinds of slave trading? Why couldn't the King stop the Portuguese? What was the most important thing to remember in the fall of the Kongo Kingdom?
36. Pretend speech bubbles are above the heads of two people standing on the right in the Figure 26. What might they be saying/thinking?

Why was the Kongo Princess burned at the stake?
37. Watch The Young Noble Girl That Revived An African Empire https://youtu.be/HinY1xNlDyY 8:03
38. Why was the Kongo Princess able to attract thousands of followers from all walks of life, as a teenager and in her early twenties?
39. Some historians compare Beatriz Kimpa Vita to the French Joan of Arc. Why? Research similarities and differences.

Could diamonds be forever?
40. How many countries in Africa? Locate Angola. Where was the Kingdom of Kongo located in the past?
41. Africa is a country or continent. **True or False.** Learn the countries of Africa in this game. https://online.seterra.com/en/vgp/3163
42. Find out more about Blood diamonds at Geology.com here https://geology.com/articles/blood-diamonds.shtml
43. Listen to Kanye West (Ft. Jay-Z) – Diamonds from Sierra Leone (Lyrics on Screen) up to 2:10. before Jay-z. https://youtu.be/e6vn5B5nL-Q Does Kanye wear bling? Why/Why not? Highlight the lyrics that link with diamonds. Then write your own Angola poem/rap.
44. Pretend speech bubbles are above the heads of two people in the fish market photo. What might they be saying/thinking before the photo?

What was the Assiento de Negroes?
45. How were companies able to trade in human beings? Why would they want to become involved in this trade in the first place?
46. Why did Assientos stop? Why don't we know exact numbers shipped?
47. Find out how wealthy Britain became upon Black enslavement. BBC Wealth Created by British Slave Traders https://www.bbc.co.uk/bitesize/clips/z4ss34j 1:47

To raid or not to raid; is that the question?
48. How did the guns-for-cycle increase enslavement?
49. Find out the meanings of these words, *dilemma, catch 22, quandary*.
50. How have Eurocentric historians used a few 'greedy African rulers' for their own purposes?

What is the fallacy of Africans selling each other?
51. Define fallacy. Give three reasons why this particular fallacy exists.
52. Learn about Olaudah Equiano at the BBC http://www.bbc.co.uk/history/historic_figures/equiano_olaudah.shtml and https://equiano.uk/
53. Read BBC Ethics http://www.bbc.co.uk/ethics/slavery/ Give three reasons why the Spanish thought chattel enslavement was justified.
54. Why do Eurocentric historians say 'Africans sold each other'? Write a short paragraph to explain your thoughts.

Floating tombs- a way to die?
55. Are Figure 33 and quotes 10-11 primary or secondary sources?
56. What does bias mean? If a source is biased, does that mean it has no use at all?
57. Quote 10: How many enslaved died? Why? Who wrote this source? What is their job? Is this source biased?
58. Quote 11: What city/country does the person come from who wrote this? Is it biased? Is that a good thing or a bad thing?
59. Figure 33: In 1788, an Act of Parliament was passed which limited the number of enslaved that could be carried on a ship according to its tonnage. What is tonnage?

How many were raced across the Atlantic?
60. Locate and label all the places mentioned on this page. Which are cities, countries or continents?
61. Look at Figure 37. Draw all the routes from 'First known region of embarkation' to the port of Buenos Ayres (Río De La Plata) on a map.
62. Explain the differences between European and trans-American (inter-American) slave routes.
63. Where did 38% of captives come from? Now make pie charts from Figure 37.

Who was sold to the highest bidder?
64. What is an auction?
65. What happened to African women, children and men once they landed in Río de la Plata?
66. Write a short poem about how the Africans might have felt during the auction. Use a thesaurus to find synonyms.
67. Read Quote 12 and the information again. Why were the enslaved 'seasoned?' What does it mean?
68. Translate the Spanish auction advert into English. What have you found out about chattel enslavement?

Chapter 4

What was the Spanish invention of racism?	32
Who was white but not quite?	33
How to buy whiteness and be perfectly white	34
How the castas divided and controlled	35
How African blood is triumphant	36
What was the myth of African violence?	37
What were the Piezas de Indias?	38
Chapter 4 Activities	39-40

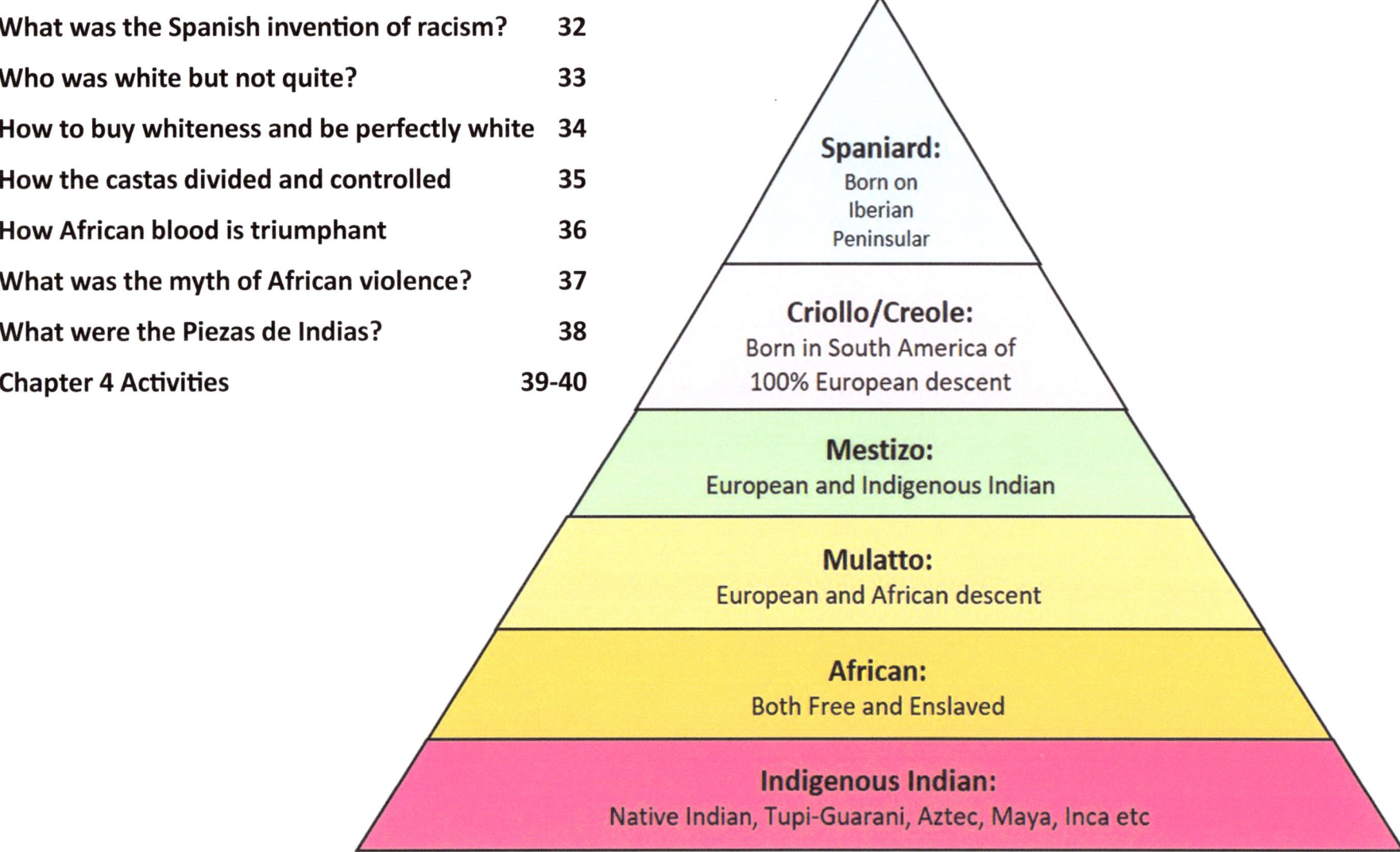

Figure 39: Spanish Racial Pyramid System

What was the Spanish invention of racism?

The Iberian Peninsula included Spain, Portugal, Andorra (southern France), and Gibraltar. This region had been conquered and controlled by the Muslims between 711 and 1492. Muslims built the tourist attractions of the Mosque in Cordoba and Palace of Alhambra in Spain. Muslim rule eventually fell and then Spain became obsessed with **'blood purity'**.

At first, this was religious purity because Indian, Arab, African or Jewish peoples practised different religions. Their blood was 'unclean'; known as *"limpieza de sangre"*. Skin colour was the easiest way for whites to believe African peoples were innately inferior to them. Over time, 'blood purity' included imaginary differences between whiteness and blackness.

Figure 40: From a Spanish Man and a Black Woman, a Mulatto, 1760–70. Denver Art Museum Collection

Later on, those imaginary differences led to colour prejudice, negative stereotypes and racial domination. Simply put, this is the invention of racism against African peoples so Europeans could justify continued exploitation and enslavement. Remember that racism is a system of advantage based on skin colour and unequal power relationships. As Dr Jack D Forbes, a Native American Historian pointed out, 'a slave cannot be a slave unless he was denied, – substantially or even totally his rights as a subject'. Thus, **racism only benefits whites.** The Spanish ensured that whites had all the legal rights and advantages under their *Sistema de Castas.*

In the *Sistema de Castas*, children of African mothers and Spanish fathers were named "mulattoes". "Mulatto" is a Spanish word for mule. A mule is a mixture of a male donkey and female horse, born for hard work. *Casta* meant "mixed-race". In English, *Casta* is Caste, and used to describe mixed-race people as "half-caste". Today, "half-caste" and the other Spanish racial inventions, are '...offensive, designed only to exclude people from any rights enjoyed by white people', concluded historian, Professor George Reid Andrews (1980).

Sistema de Castas included **limited or no access** for Black people to: schooling and education; occupations and professions; law and justice; money and finance; health and medical; land and property leading to a lack of intergenerational wealth; marriage choices and families, that whites enjoyed naturally. This is the act of **discrimination** and **segregation**. Remember apartheid? An extreme example of **white privileges**, the legacy of which operates as structural racism today. Whites did not and do not have to think about their natural privileges, but Black people always have to consider their blackness and movement at any time, in any space and any place.

Who was white but not quite?

Sistema de Castas was the legal racial system based on the superiority of one group of people over another. Shown in these paintings describing which mixtures were white but not quite, and that some racial mixtures were better than others. It was a means of control.

Each *casta* image displayed an 'imagined' family: a mother, a father, and one or two children that bore strange names. They were divided into sixteen racial groupings. Those at the top were white with partners who were white but not quite. Darker shades in the middle. Blacks and Indians at the bottom in deteriorating surroundings and clothes showing the class that they supposedly belonged to. However, assigning *castas* was not that simple.

Historian, Dr Rebecca Earle's research described a sixteenth century priest's confusion: 'a woman initially described as "lora", a term roughly translatable as "brownish", was later labelled first as "white", and then as both "Morena" (dark) and "Indian-coloured."

Dividing the races along a colour spectrum attempted to identify ancestry and avoid impure blood. The *casta* paintings were symbols of families at home or at work in mostly harmonious relationships, for the amusement of those back in the Iberian Peninsula. Europeans could engage in their romantic exotic fantasies, hanging on their walls as 'art'. Dr Earle said that the *castas* were nothing more than '…flights of imagination.'

Figure 41: Casta painting showing 16 hierarchically arranged, mixed-race groupings. Real Academia Española de la Lengua, Madrid. Perhaps used as a chart to determine their children's 'destination' – similar to reading a map!

The truth is that the *castas* displayed persuasive psychological messages of colonial control but at the same time suggested racial harmony, according to some experts. They were based on religious ethicised variations of Jesus, Mary, and child, the Holy family but also stressed the differences between blackness and whiteness.

An interesting point was made by African American historian, Dr Tekla Ali Johnson, who said that, **'it was in fact upon these mixed-race people that the workings of domination depended. Although they occasionally operated with fellow Africans as resistors, "mulattoes" more frequently helped whites sustain slavery and the oppression of other Africans.'**

How to buy whiteness and be perfectly white

Passing. Small drops of white blood put a person above someone who was not 'pure white.' It was the huge numbers of mulattos or the white mixed-race people, that worried the Spanish Crown, passing as white Spaniards. For example:

1. A Spaniard and Castizo child is three-quarter white Spanish.
2. A Spaniard and Indian child is also three-quarter white Spanish.
3. A child born from both 1 and 2 can pass as a white Spaniard, **perfectly white**.

Therefore, Mestizos' grand or great grandchildren were not only regarded as Spanish but as **perfectly white**. Perfectly white people could buy a 'Certificate of Whiteness', under the Gracias al Sacar 1795 Decree, to prove that they were 'white'!

Figure 42: De Españoi y Mestiza Castiza by Miguel Cabrera (Spaniard and Mestiza with Castiza child)

The truth is that few people knew about the bizarre Gracias al Sacar Decree. It is unsurprising that many people could not remember who their ancestors were. Some people who were legally born *castas* became 'perfectly white' as they were well-off, with lighter skins, and denied their African heritage. Money can buy whiteness.

Many 'pass' as Spaniards who in their own hearts know they are Mulatos, and those known to be such are sometimes, more leniently, called Pardoes just as Negroes are sometimes called Morenos.
Quote 13: Excerpted from Pedro Alonso O'Crouley, 1774

In truth, many Indians and Africans were taught to despise themselves and their cultures. For a better life, they had to be or desired to be 'white'. Some Indian groups or their descendants adapted white habits, clothes and the Spanish language. Black people were meant to mix in with whites until they, '...eventually disappeared, taking their primitive culture with them', according to Anthropology Professor Dr Peter Wade. Yet this racist notion failed because African blood, when mixed, is still triumphant. However, after generations of psychological whitewashing, convincing most Black people to think of themselves as inferior beings with the associated lack of self-esteem and self-worth were more successful.

The *Sistema de Castas* legally barred people of African descent or darker skins from obtaining higher paying occupations and trades, plus other social and moral controls, without a Certificate of Whiteness; unless it suited the white elites to 'allow' them these 'privileges', called tokenism today. However, those limitations in professions and occupations still remain for most ordinary Black people. Not only due to systematic racism but self-limitation due to the psychological effects and legacies of centuries of white supremacy.

How the castas divided and controlled

The Spanish Crown not only created divisions between white, Black, and Indian peoples, but between each *casta* level as well.

Firstly: the truth is that the upper *castas* (1-8) were **Spanish men who had power over all women and their babies,** leaving the African, Indian and Mixed-race men powerless, a metaphor for domination by Spain.

Secondly: as a 'divide and control' system. According to Native American Anthropologist and Historian, Dr Jack D. Forbes, the upper *castas* who had lighter skin tones, *mulattos, mestizas, castizas* were used to control the lower *castas* who were darker-skinned. 'The partially-excluded *castas*', explained the anthropologist, 'were used to control the masses'.

1. From a Spanish man and an Indian woman is born a *Mestiza*
2. From a Spanish man and a Mestiza woman is born a *Castiza*
3. From a Spanish man and a Castiza woman is born a *Spaniard*
4. From a Spanish man and a Black woman is born a *Mulata*
5. From a Spanish man and a Mulata woman is born a *Morisca*
6. From a Spanish man and a Morisca woman is born an *Albina*
7. From a Spanish man and an Albina woman is born a *Torna-atras*
8. From a Spanish man and a Throwback woman is born a *Tente en al aire*
9. From a Black man and an Indian woman is born a *China Cambuja*
10. From a Chino Cambujo man and an Indian woman is born a *Loba*
11. From a Lobo man and an Indian woman is born an *Albarazado*
12. From an Albarazado man and a Mestiza woman is born a *Barcino*
13. From an Indian man and a Barcina woman is born a *Zambaiga*
14. From a Castizo man and a Mestiza woman is born a *Chamizo*
15. From a Mestizo man and an Indian woman is born a *Coyote*
16. Heathen Indians

Figure 43: Typical Casta Paintings Captions: Miguel Cabrera's 1763 series: **(These words are not appropriate for use today).**

Thirdly: the divide and control system between the *castas* resulted in the belief that lighter skin was better than darker skin. This led to lighter skinned people being viewed as more trustworthy and 'superior' to the darker skinned people. This is an aspect of colonial mentality, called colourism. The effect of lighter skin shades on ordinary white people and officials resulted in favouritism. Today, an industry of skin-lightening creams and pills have sprung up. Most of which are dangerous to health and some are banned.

Fourthly: to divide and control Africans even further, Black people were displayed as violent and aggressive. There were over one hundred paintings in sets of sixteen. In each set, one out of the sixteen, showed a scene of domestic violence with African women or men as the perpetrator. This only served to reinforce the colourism stereotype which became 'scientific fact' for white people in subsequent centuries. For instance, favouritism towards lighter skin Black people and darker skinned people, seen as violent.

The Spanish *Sistema de Castas* were successful as a 'divide and control' system to benefit only the descendants of the whites, or those who could 'pass' as white. The whites used the upper levels of the mixed-race *castas* who were the partially-excluded from society, to control the lower *castas*, and in particular, keeping 'pure Indians' and 'pure Africans' at the bottom of any human rights. This is, perhaps, how the Europeans divided the African and Indian peoples and controlled the generations of white, African, and Indian admixtures within the colony.

How African blood is triumphant

No. 7 *Casta*, torna-atras is: from Albino (or mulatto) and Spaniard, a Black boy is born. This meant 'return backwards', or in English 'a throwback'. This is two whites producing a Black baby, a 'throwback' child to distant Black or Indian ancestors that might return by the subsequent generations, and therefore a dilution of Spanish purity.

The union of an Albino with a Spaniard was actually seen as a step backward; back towards an African heritage, instead of forward to a white European future. On the other hand, this colonial fear shows how African blood is triumphant throughout the generations. The painting suggested that one of the last generations of a Black and Spanish racial mixture created, a return to 'Blackness', according to the experts.

Figure 44: Andrés de Islas, De Español, y Alvina, nace, torna-atras [From a Spaniard and an Albina is Born a Throwback], 1774. Museo de América, Madrid in Spain.

The truth is, however, that it was more common for two Black parents to have an albino child, which in the eighteenth century, the French referred to as 'pigmentless human'. In the Torna-Atras painting, the child:

- is held and dressed in luxurious clothing, similar to the father. So, the *casta* becomes acceptable to the Spaniards.
- has a coat on like his father so they will go out together in public. Meaning that the Spaniard is not ashamed of the *casta* if they dress and behave as whites.
- looks at the Spanish father, as *castas* and Black peoples must take direction from white Spaniards for guidance.
- although the child displays his blackness; his back is turned away from his Albino mother; represented as leaving the past of enslavement behind, looking towards whites for their future.

Yet, the truth is that these harmonious paintings are not real families, only Spain's exotic imaginings and fantasies. A form of racist propaganda by the colonial elite. Clearly showing their racialised and gender attitudes and beliefs. No doubt, these images affected both ordinary Black and white people, only to perpetuate and sustain racialised attitudes. However, due to the huge numbers of admixtures by Spanish men, the truth is, these were severe warnings about dangers of white dilution. African blood might re-appear in subsequent generations, even if their appearance seemed white. As African Argentine University Professor Erika Edwards said about porteños in 2003, 'Though many have white skin, their veins flow of Black blood'.

What was the myth of African violence?

The *castas* displayed varying clothing types from wealthy to rags, food and drink, facial expressions, and positions. The son or daughter in the *castas* is usually in the middle of the parents and becomes one of the parents in the next scene. The lower the *casta*, the more the surroundings, clothing, and expressions, deteriorate.

Domestic violence is shown in one *casta* out of the sixteen and displayed an African person as the perpetrator. The violent *castas* are in direct contrast to the peaceful and calm of the Spanish man combinations, to highlight the differences. Figure 45 shows:

- An African woman in simple clothes with an ugly expression, is in the kitchen beating the Spanish man with a cooking tool. His hat has been knocked off and is on the floor behind him. The woman obviously has the upper hand. This perhaps leads to the damaging stereotype today of the so-called, 'aggressive Black woman'.

- A white Spanish man in uniform, representing Spanish authority, is unable to control the African woman as he grabs her other arm. He is standing by the open window with trees in the background as opposed to the woman who is beside the kitchen.

- In contrast, there is a fruit basket on the floor in front of the woman, with such items listed on the wall above. Typically, 'Blacks and mulattoes could not sell chickens, fruits, and vegetables, …' according to historian, Professor Douglas Richmond.

- A mulata (female mulatto) child, representing the *casta* population, stands in the middle alongside the father, as the mediator attempting to stop the violence. The father is unable to control the woman. Perhaps the mulata has a better chance.

Figure 45: From Spanish and Black; Mulata is born. Fruits of the country; Mulata is born. 1744 by Andres islands

The control and divide system were represented in these violent *castas*. The mulata represented the control of the Spanish authority whilst caught between the white Spanish and the African Other. Experts agreed that the violence displayed was associated with 'blackness'. Although these may have represented Spanish fantasy, they contributed towards the violent and aggressive stereotypes of Black people, the legacy of which still remains.

What were the Piezas de Indias?

A unit of measurement. Law Professor, Dr Agustin Parise, from Maastricht University, outlined the names used for captives in the Río de la Plata area. Dr Parise stated these 'terms were especially violent and denoted no respect for human life'.

Pieza is a male or female enslaved, between fifteen and thirty years, without vices, and with all their teeth. The number of piezas in the shipment, the money stated in the *Assientos,* and taxes collected by royal officials, were all recorded using these terms, wrote Dr Parise.

Figure 46: Slavery in chains

These monetary units are not real, but used to convert human parts and labour into money terms.
- **Cabeza de Negro** (Black's Head): **Cabeza de Esclavo** (Head of Slave) described any Black slave, male or female;
- **Un Cuarto** (Quarter), **Media Pieza** (Half Piece): defects in age, stature, and/or health;
- **Cuatro Quintos de Pieza** (Four-Fifths of a Piece): 'defects';
- **Tres (three) Piezas of Indians:** one ton of Black individuals;
- **Negro Bozal** (Black Muzzle): recently arrived from Africa; meaning wild or savage.
- **Ladino**: a slave who had been in Americas for at least a year;
- **Negro de Asta** (Spear Black): a cabeza de negro that reached the height of the spear;

As well as companies and organisations making fortunes for Spain, Britain, Portugal, France, and the Netherlands economies, individuals gained fortunes whilst promoting themselves as 'devoted Catholics' whilst carrying out 'charitable works' back in their respective countries!

In 2019, the United Nations Human Rights on People of African Descent in Argentina, highlighted, amongst other aspects, offensive modern-day insults such as "working like a negro" and "working black", "look at the black", and "girl/boy from the slums," and "Negro". The UN **'…urges the government to carry out awareness-raising programmes to prevent use of words and expressions which are demeaning to African descendants.'**

Chapter 4 Activities

What was the Spanish invention of racism?
69. Read more about Muslim Spain at BBC Religions Muslim Spain (711-1492) https://tinyurl.com/y6wx2ac2
70. Look at the painting. Answer these questions.

    a. What is the boy doing?
    b. Why is he bowing to the man?
    c. What is the mother doing?
    d. What is the difference in their clothes?
    e. What is the room like? Why?
    f. What overall impression does this painting show?

71. Describe Sistema de Castas in three sentences.
72. Visit, The Apartheid Museum https://www.apartheidmuseum.org/ and https://www.bbc.co.uk/archive/apartheid-in-south-africa/zh96kmn /
73. Who is this famous person? https://youtu.be/jgQBoXsxr8w / https://www.youtube.com/watch?v=lh7yZZN2oz0 Research more information and prepare a biography about his achievements. What you admire the most about him?

Who was white but not quite? This link displays a larger *casta* image https://commons.wikimedia.org/wiki/Template:PD-old
74. Which rows show families with the least clothing and shoes? Why?

    a. What differences do you notice between the settings on the top and bottom rows?
    b. Where are the children positioned within each family on the top two rows? Why do you think they are shown in that position?
    c. The father is at a distance from the Black child hugging the white mother in No.7. Why?
    d. Why is the African woman in No. 15 shown cooking? Why does the father in No. 10 carry a jug of alcohol? Which *casta*?
    e. What does 'heathen' mean? Which *casta* or skin colour is shown as 'heathen'? Why?

How to buy whiteness and be perfectly white
75. What is colour prejudice?
76. Do you think that 'Passing' mixed race people were accepted by their neighbours as 'real' white people?
77. What is the difference between feeling proud or feeling superior?
78. Racism is illegal in UK but it still happens. Read, take the quiz and watch the video at BBC - What was the Race Relations Act? https://www.bbc.co.uk/newsround/46310188

How the Castas divided and controlled

79. What were the consequences of being white, Black, or mixed-race?
80. How were different *castas* used against each other?
81. Look at Figure 43. Where do the names of children come from? Plants, Zoological, both, something else? What they mean and why did the Spanish use such names?

How African blood is triumphant

82. Why would Torna-Atras be a concern to the white Spanish people?
83. Find out more about Albinism at Albinism Fellowship https://www.albinism.org.uk/about-albinism/
84. Watch the video- I'm Black, Even with Albinism | BORN DIFFERENT 5:00 https://youtu.be/gYjlFu0pltw

What was the myth of African violence?

85. Describe the role of the child?
86. Do violent *casta* paintings show the dangers of women in general, or focus specifically on Black women?
87. Why would *castas* show Africans as violent? What is your opinion? How does the myth of African (Black) violence in the past relate to society today?

What were Piezas de Indias?

88. Look up the definitions of 'derogatory', 'denigrate', 'respect', and 'tolerance'.

    a. Why do people denigrate others who may be different?
    b. Why do people treat other human beings as objects?
    c. How can people respect each other?

89. Have you ever made fun of someone, called someone names, or witnessed others doing that, because of a cultural trait or they are different to you? How would you improve your reaction if it happened again? How would you behave if you saw someone calling another person a name?

Chapter 5

Who were the gauchos and what did they invent?	42
Why was the Bottomless Bucket misappropriated?	43
What was the Tasajo slavery trail to Cuba?	44
There weren't any plantations here…	45
What was the cycle of low status labour?	46
How fashionable were Black children?	47
Chapter 5 Activities	48

Figure 47: Ostrich hunting on the pampas using bolas 1870

Who were the gauchos and what did they invent?

Gaucho means cowboy. They were Africans, Meztisos and Indians who herded hundreds of thousands of cattle, sheep and horses on the Pampas countryside. They made cattle hides, saddles, waxes and meats. Many were also payadores (singers) with guitars. The 1789 Royal Real Cidula Law stated that, 'The first ... occupation of slaves must be agriculture and other field works', according to Law Professor, Dr Agustin Parise.

Gauchos wore slouchy hats and silk handkerchiefs around their necks. They wore 'hundred day shirts meaning that they threw it away and got a clean one...', according to A. L. Lloyd (History Today 1951), 'every hundred days'. They wore chiripas around the waist which were blankets worn as loose-fitting trousers, and had large knives inside their belts, for butchering cattle. Wool ponchos were worn in cold weather and high-heeled boots.

Figure 48: Painting of Gauchos

Eurocentric experts presented as 'scientific fact', that Africans had no intelligence because as captives, they were passive and inferior. In contrast, anthropologist Andrew Sluyter's examination of the evidence for lassoing cattle, ' **... suggested that those inventors were actually of African origin**', and that **'in Senegambia, herders used lassos to restrain rebellious bulls whilst running or standing'.**

Long before cowboys were popular in western movies, gauchos rode horses using lassos and boladoras (bolas) to catch leopards, jaguars and ostriches. Bolas are three balls of stone attached to plaited ropes, whirled over their heads and thrown at the animals' legs or necks. Boladoras are now sold as tourist souvenirs.

By the end of the nineteenth century, the gauchos were whitened and exorcised of their Indian and Black heritage. The Pampas had been fenced off into huge cattle ranches, *estancias.* The once free-spirited gauchos were criminalised; forced into the

Figure 49: Gauchos hunting Leopards

military; into reservations or worked as peon labourers. They were subjected to *historia negra negada.* Today, however, gauchos have become the romanticised symbols of white "authentic nostalgic" memories.

How was the bottomless bucket misappropriated?

Outside Buenos Ayres, gauchos herded cattle on the vast Pampas plains. Anthropology Professor Arnold Strickon said that, 'slavery and ranching did not mix', because it 'was obviously impractical to allow slaves to herd cattle without close, constant supervision by whites'.

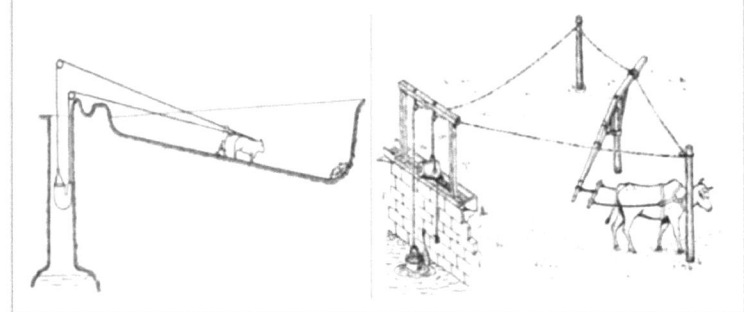

Figure 50: Cross section of similar early water lifting devices using animals and buckets.

This stereotype is another eurocentric myth. Before the fifteenth century, cattle herding and agriculture were sources of wealth for the Senegambians in Africa. Law Professor, Dr Agustin Parise confirmed that, 'In 1766 Buenos Aires, the Cabildo [Town Hall] alerted that the Black slaves were the only agriculturists'. Furthermore, research undertaken by Dr Andrew Sluyter at Buenos Aires Archives, researches of the census and the Voyages Transatlantic Database in 2015, uncovered:

Lassoing cattle and the water-lifting device were adapted to the Pampas by captive Africans

- 1402 Senegambians out of 2,175 that landed in the Río de la Plata between 1800 and 1806, went to the rural Pampas. Dr Sluyter's results showed that, 'a cattle herder of African birth may well have introduced the balde sin fondo to the Pampas', and that it was, *'based on his [Senegambians] experience herding cattle across the Sahel, from the valley of the Gambia, Senegal, or Niger River into the southern fringes of the Sahara'.* The balde sin fondo or bottomless bucket was adapted to provide cattle with drinking water which the Pampas lacked. This helped the cattle rapidly multiply into the hundreds of thousands in later decades.

- The balde sin fondo is described by Dr Sluyter as, *'a long narrow skin bag, open at both ends, with one thick rope that lifted the bucket and a thin rope that held the bottom closed. When it was lifted out of the well, the thin rope opened the bottom and water would spill into a chute. Then fall into a drinking trough.'*

The problem was that the bottomless bucket was misappropriated by official Carlos Pellegrini in 1853 as identified in Dr Sluyter's research. Pellegrini attributed the balde sin fondo creation to a Spaniard named Vicente Lanuza, who said he invented it, and that has been repeated as a fact ever since. Dr Sluyter's research showed that it was more likely the enslaved and their descendants' water lifting devices that contributed towards Argentinian nation-building. However, the enslaved Africans, *meztisos* and Indians' life as agricultural gauchos became *historia negra negada*, erased and whitewashed from Argentinian memory.

What was the Tasajo slavery trail to Cuba?

Tasajo is sun-dried salted and smoked beef from cows. The reek of tasajo saturated the port city. The city was described as, '…ditches filled with blood instead of water…' by a nineteenth century traveller, in Dr Andrew Sluyter's 2012 research. Tasajo was produced and eaten by the African enslaved not only in Buenos Ayres, but in Cuba and Brazil as well. Historian George Reid Andrews explained that Black men worked as Achuradoras in the Río de la Plata slaughterhouses:

> *… salvaging tripe, lung, organs, and diseased meat from slaughtered animals. The achuradoras then sold this cast-off meat to blacks and poor whites who could not afford anything better.* George Reid Andrews (1980)

Figure 51: Tasajo (beef jerky) in Argentina

Poverty led tasjao to become a firm favourite because it lasted for months after slaughter in tropical climates. Today it is called beef jerky (charque in Brazil). It was 'served as the main source of nourishment for the enslaved labourers who worked on coffee and sugar cane plantations', claimed Professor Thales Pereira. Alongside the European slave trade, Dr Sluyter investigated Tasajo Trails to Cuba:

1. From Spain to Africa. Traded in slaves; onwards to Cuba and back with sugar, tobacco, and coffee.
2. Direct trading of goods with Cuba, without slave trading.
3. Spanish flour, wine, aguardiente, olive oil, paper, cork, textiles, dried fruit, and shoes, to Buenos Ayres. Tasajo was collected for Cuba. Once in Cuba, sugar, coffee, tobacco, and hides were loaded back towards Spain.

> *…a Liverpool (England) ship called Scamander that arrived in Buenos Ayres with general cargo valued at £12,966 and left for Havana (Cuba) with £1,365 worth of jerked beef in 1830.*
>
> Quote 14: Return of the British trade within the Consulate of Buenos Ayres during the Half Year ending the 30th June 1829

Tasajo brought great wealth to Buenos Ayres but it declined when enslavement was outlawed. However, most porteños had opportunities for intergenerational wealth. That is, passing down any wealth to the next generation. For Black people, there was little or no chance of inheriting or passing on wealth or land to the next generation resulting in the racial wealth gap of today. Furthermore, because Tasajo evoked the stench of slavery and Black people, it was part of *historia negra negada*, erased and forgotten from Argentina's nation-building and memory.

There weren't any plantations here...

is another popular Argentine phrase. Another white myth, used to distance Argentina from the slave trade. Sugar cane was introduced in the seventeenth century, mostly in the rural areas of Tucumán, Salta, and Jujuy provinces, where many Black people still live today. Around 64% of Tucumán citizens are of West African origin. At one time, Tucumán had 15 sugar mills, 3 in Jujuy and 2 in Salta according to the experts.

Following the collapse of the encomienda system, many of the Spanish encomenderos and their descendants worked in the *estancias* and plantation mills. But for rural people, working on sugar plantations meant:

1. Killing off people already living on the land to make way for the white 'civilised' Europeans.
2. Selling and appropriating Indian land into cattle estancias, sugar mills and plantations.
3. Claiming survivors as uncivilised savages, rebels, or enemies of the state, and using them as cheap labour.
4. Forcing survivors to pay rent for living on their own land.
5. Working at the sugar mills or plantations in order to pay the rent for living on their land.
6. Increasing costs for basic goods so the workers remained in debt and needed to work at the mills.
7. Cheating workers by dishonest weighing practices.
8. Paying wages as credit vouchers that could only be used in the mill shops.
9. Spending a lifetime working off the debt that kept increasing, whilst making the owners wealthy.
10. Abusive landowners, merchants, and officials collaborated in these exploitation practices.

Figure 52: Cutting Sugar Cane. Museo de la Industria Azucarera.

Sugar cane was a [virtual] El Dorado, claimed Señor Pillado, the chief of the Agricultural Department, because the production leapt from '…24,000 tons in 1884, to 75,000 in 1894.' Quote 15: Ricardo Pillado (1906). Politica Comercial Argentina. Buenos Ayres

Rather than an informal system where labourers had choices and worked under supposedly harmonious conditions, as some historians believed, debt peonage was a legally recognized labour force. Whippings, stocks, or prison, were used as enforcement for failure to show work registration, working slowly, running away or vagrancy, or scandalous behaviour for women (!) according to the experts. However, whether actual or threatened or psychological, peonage and debt labour needed violence to keep it going.

What was the cycle of low status labour?

In the 1770s, those with a drop of African blood were legally barred from higher status urban jobs. Far from being victims and inferior, the truth is that the enslaved were capable of working at any form of labour, despite being regulated to 'the least desirable, most degrading, unhealthiest, and worst paying jobs …', said Professor George Reid Andrews (1980).

Hiring or Renting out: Some slave owners rented out their skilled captives and artisans for payment. Owners kept most of the cash income to keep up their lifestyle. The rest of the cash was allowed to be kept by the enslaved.

Figure 53: The Sellers Lithograph by Hipólito Bacle in 19th century Buenos Ayres

Domestics: Women worked as cooks, teachers to slavers' children, wet nurses, maids, laundresses, washerwomen. Black vendors sold pastries, empanadas, dusters, and dairy products. Men worked as servants, butlers, and coachmen. 'So widespread was the phenomenon, that the elegantly turned-out manservant was a frequent feature of fiction and cartoons from the period', wrote Reid Andrews (1979). Similarly, Black women were numerous in white houses that they became caricatures in Spanish media. A caricature exaggerates facial and physical features to make people mock and laugh at them.

Artisans: 'The Black women and men in Buenos Ayres demonstrated an obvious entrepreneurial capacity', noted Reid Andrews. 'They were tailors, cobblers, blacksmiths, masons, and pest exterminators'. Black men were seamen, dockworkers, keepers of pulperias, bull fighters, fishermen, musicians, but they were barred from becoming higher level artisans and joining, for example, the shoemakers of Buenos Aires. Evidence from records in the Cabildo (Town Hall) pointed out that, 'a mulatto named Ambrosio, was whipped in the central plaza in Catamarca province for proving that he knew how to read and write'!

Within the urban city, artisans and domestics were vital in the development of Buenos Ayres as the capital and bustling city of today. The problem, identified Reid Andrews, was that **'the low occupational status, and low racial status reinforced each other, in a circle that became impossible to break'**. Today, laws mitigate against discrimination and racism, but economic inferiority for most Black people still exists leading to the lack of intergenerational wealth of today.

How fashionable were Black children?

Black children were mainly domestics in provinces, such as Córdoba (founded 1573), Tucumán (1565) as well as Buenos Ayres amongst others. In these areas, '… no high aspiring Buenos Ayres household would be without their staggering numbers of enslaved domestics', said Historian, Professor George Reid Andrews.

In 2014, University Sociologist, Dr Edward Telles wrote about a North American in Buenos Ayres from 1817, and recalled how, 'no respectable Argentine woman would think of going to mass without a black maidservant to carry her rug and attend to her during the services'. Samuel Haigh, a British explorer, confirmed this in 1837, that '…fashionable ladies may then be seen in groups followed by their Black or mulatto girls carrying carpet rugs of the most brilliant colours for them to kneel upon, as the churches have no pews, and are all paved either with brick or stone'.

Figure 54: Enslaved Domestic. Lithograph, Bacle-Moulin: "Ladies in the morning", Buenos Aires, 1833. In Hernán F. Pas (2011) La seducción de las imágenes. El ingreso de la litografia y los nuevos modos de publicidad en Latinoamérica. Caracol 10.10.11606 v0i2p10-41. Image page 31.

Dr. Kara Schultz's research calculated the number of children landed between 1612 and 1632, as shown in Figure 55. Children were labelled as *muleques* who were under twelve, counted as half a slave; suckling infants were known as *crias* who were free of duties.

Date of arrival in Buenos Aires	Ship Name	Region of Slave Purchase	Known captives landed	Number of children	Percentage of known captives landed
13 December 1612	NS de las Nieves	Angola	244	59 *muleques*	24
17 March 1613	Santa Cruz	Angola	9	2 *muleques*	22
7 January 1623	El Angel Sant Rafael	Angola	275	43 *crias*	16
3 April 1623	La Bendicion de Dios	Angola	160	32 *crias*	20
5 April 1623	NS del Rosario	Angola	116	52 *crias*	45
6 April 1623	NS de Candelaria	Angola	31	7 *crias*	23
20 April 1623	NS del Rosario	Angola	122	52 *crias*	43
3 May 1623	La Concepción	Bahia	39	7 *crias*	18
1632	Unnamed patache	Brazil	50	"many children among them"	**

Figure 55: Table of a selection of slave ships arriving in the port of Buenos Ayres with significant numbers of child captives, by Dr. Kara D. Schultz (2015) (These words are not appropriate today)

Experts estimated that children made up about 50% of all captives shipped from Luanda during the late eighteenth and early nineteenth centuries. Children could be more tightly packed into the slaving vessels.

However, the truth is, the packing of slaving vessels to match ship tonnage had nothing to do with relieving human suffering, but everything to do with maximising profit! Also, children were cheaper as little or no taxes were paid. They were easier to control physically and easier to accept their inferior position. On the other hand, Black children were status symbols for fashionable wealthy porteños.

Chapter 5 Activities

Who were the gauchos and what did they invent?
90. What clothing and tools are typical of a gaucho?
91. Draw a gaucho. Early gauchos were nomadic. What does nomadic mean? What did they use to hunt?
92. Watch National Geographic, The Way of the Gaucho https://youtu.be/GekP1ratwf4 2:03

Why was the bottomless bucket misappropriated?
93. Why was the bottomless bucket culturally misappropriated?
94. Follow Dr Sluyter's description to make a working bottomless bucket or draw one following the instructions.
95. Research and draw Egyptian water lifting devices. Compare and contrast with the bottomless bucket.

What was the tasajo slavery trail to Cuba?
96. How many varieties of jerky can you find in your local supermarket?
97. Find the three Tasajo American routes on a map, draw arrows to show the routes. Label and draw the goods that they carried.
98. Locate Liverpool and Havana in an atlas, on a globe, and calculate the distances in kilometres from Rio de la Plata.

There weren't any plantations here…
99. Compare and contrast the Encomienda and sugar mills system in a two-circle Venn diagram.
100. Read Article 23 and 24 of the Universal Declaration of Human Rights https://www.un.org/en/universal-declaration- human-rights/
101. Write an email as a human rights activist to the mill workers. Describe the rights that the workers are entitled to. Tell them what actions you will take to help them.

What was the cycle of low status labour?
102. Watch Human Rights and Business https://youtu.be/McaE4_ivM-Q 1:50 and Universal Declaration of Human Rights https://youtu.be/hTlrSYbCbHE 4:31
103. Read Equality and Human Rights https://www.equalityhumanrights.com/en/human-rights-act/article-4-freedom-slavery-and-forced-labour Which human rights have been violated regarding these workers?
104. Write an acrostic poem using the word 'freedom' written down one side, to explain what you have learned about human rights.

How fashionable were Black children?
105. What are your status symbols in the 21st century? Who is trying to impress who?
106. Write a conversation that could be happening between the enslaved boy and the two women in that room.
107. Look at Figure 55. Plot the countries named on a map arriving at Rio de la Plata.
108. Look at Region of slave purchase column on Figure 54. Make a pie chart showing the percentages from Angola, Bahia and Brazil.
109. What do you think happened to the children when they grew up?

Chapter 6

How did the enslaved resist?	**50**
What were the mutiny myths?	**51**
What were the white myths of resistance?	**52**
What were the white abolition myths?	**53**
How the blacks has kill'd the whites...	**54**
Is the price of manumission freedom?	**55**
Free or freed or freeborn or free slave?	**56**
What is the myth of the slave house?	**57**
Chapter 6 Activities	**58-59**

Figure 56: Africans fought against the slave trade on the coasts by attacking slave ships and killing their crews, 1855.

How did the enslaved resist?

Some historians argued that captives outnumbered the whites, hence, they could easily rebel. However, it was not that simple. The truth is that resistance put the captives and their families at greater risk of punishment. Enslavement was a legal institution. For example, an enslaved family would be executed if just one of them slapped their slaver.

Runaways: were a constant concern for Argentine slavers. 'The "negroes alzados, risen blacks", who fled on horseback, joined the roaming bands of gauchos desperadoes', according to historian George Reid Andrews. Dr Alex Borucki (2017) said that 'Portuguese mulattoes roamed the frontier and helped slaves to escape'. Although, it was not just about escaping abuse, but running towards family members after forced separation.

Figure 57: A Ride for Liberty – The Fugitive Slaves, *1862 Painting by Eastman Johnson*.

Small acts: work slowly, break tools, destroy cattle, feign sickness and other acts of sabotage. These acts gave way to white stereotypes of Black behaviour, particularly when captives pretended not to understand or care. The truth is that these were coping strategies.

Acts against laws: poisoning slavers; suicides; learning to read and write; free blacks helping enslaved in secret. Anthropologist, Irene Diggs wrote that, 'Slaves were known to kill their masters', and that sometimes, 'negroes abandoned their work. They went on strike.'

Networks: Freedom fighters in the Americas spread over borders through 'risen Blacks' and 'free Blacks'. In Africa, towns and villages were moved and rebuilt as mazes, with thick high walls and deep ditches; rivers were diverted away from where ships would dock.

Whitening: the *castas* resulted in the main labels of *pardo, moreno, mulatto, negro* in later decades. Eventually, they were all combined into '*trigueño*', similar to the colour of wheat, in the census. Experts such as African American Historian, Dr Tekla Johnson said that, 'Consciously or subconsciously, many free Africans sought to improve their children's life chances by moving further away from their African heritage'. However, as the decades progressed, *trigueño* was also officially dropped from the census, further perpetrating the myth of, — *aquí no hay negroes,* and that Blacks have supposedly 'disappeared'.

Eurocentric historians have argued about the lack of rebellions, but the Schomburg Center in Black Culture showed otherwise. The truth is that:

1. 'Written records document how Africans on shore attacked more than a hundred ships',
2. '...over 420 revolts have been recorded in slavers' papers and they do not represent the totality...'
3. rebellions '...driving up slaving and insurance costs'.

'Approximately one slave ship in ten experienced some form of African resistance,' confirmed Slavery and Remembrance.org.

'...55 mutinies between 1699 and 1845 and of 250 documented cases of rebellion at sea', calculated Maghan Keita, an African American University Historian, and that 'revolts broke out at the beginning of the voyage when the ship was at anchor or not far from the coast of Africa'.

> The first kind confifts of infurrections on the part of the flaves. Some of thefe frequently attempted to rife, but were prevented, (Wilfon, Town, Trotter, Newton, Dalrymple, Ellifon,) others rofe, but were quelled, (Ellifon, Newton, Falconbridge,) and others rofe, and fucceeded, killing almoft all the whites : (Falconbridge and Town).—Mr. Town fays, that inquiring of the flaves into the caufe of thefe infurrections, he has been afked, *what bufinefs he had to carry them from their country. They had wives and children, whom they wanted to be with.*

Quote 16: An abstract of the evidence delivered before a select committee of the House of Commons in the years 1790 and 1791

What were the mutiny myths?

Figure 58: Representation of an insurrection on board a Slave Ship. From the Schomburg Center in Black Culture. New York Public Library

> a favourable opportunity, failed away with them. His veffel however was, by the direction of Providence, driven back to the coaft from whence it had fet fail, and was obliged to caft anchor on the very fpot where this act of treachery had been committed. At this time two other Englifh veffels were lying in the fame river. The natives, ever fince the tranfaction, had determined to retaliate. They happened, at this juncture, to be prepared. They accordingly boarded the three veffels, and, having made themfelves mafters of them, they killed moft of their crews. The few who efcaped to tell the tale, were obliged to take refuge in a neigh-

Quote 16: "The captain of an English ship had enticed several of the natives on board..." Observations on the slave trade from the coast of Guinea, during a voyage made in 1787 and 1788 from Recovered Histories

> Befides inftances of flaves refufing to eat, with the view of deftroying themfelves, and dying in confequence of it, thofe *of their going mad*, are confirmed by Town, and of their *jumping overboad*, or attempting to do it, by Town, Millar, Ellifon, and Hall.

Quote 16: An abstract of the evidence delivered before a select committee of the House of Commons in the years 1790 and 1791

What were the white myths of resistance?

Historian George Andrew Reid 1980's research claimed that Spanish historians thought the enslaved were *'treated mildly'*. Not as cruel as the British, French or Portuguese slave owners! Eurocentric historians said that:

- porteño owners were 'kind to their slaves'
- slaves 'were comparatively well treated by their masters'
- 'slavery at Buenos Ayres is perfect freedom compared …to other nations'
- 'not as harsh as elsewhere'
- 'gladly and happily served their white masters'

Figure 59: Black man being whipped by public flogger in a town square; onlookers, others waiting to be flogged. soldiers guarding prisoners 1860s: Many floggers had little choice.

These are delusions. Evidence of numerous runaways and unjustified whippings for no reasons, proved that the captives were far from being 'treated mildly', according to Dr Lyman Johnson's study of manumissions records. Avoiding violence and racialised oppression meant some of the enslaved 'acted happy.' That was a fact of life. But in the white man's imagination, captives did not want freedom, and preferred enslavement because they were, 'treated mildly'! After all, it was the white people's duty, to look after Black people until they became 'civilised' even if they were free. This patronising attitude is called the 'white man's burden'.

Perhaps, individual personal social interactions were seen as 'kind', but the truth is that, this disregards the power imbalance. Furthermore, the fear of violence and inferiority complexes were psychologically ingrained. Discrimination caused additional stresses that whites did not have to think about in their daily lives. Black codes banned African names and religions; higher paid jobs, education, certain clothing and foods, jewellery, parts of the city, and so on. This is hardly being 'treated mildly'!

White myths attempt to lessen the brutality of enslavement, not improve the life of the captives!

The enslaved were also played off against each other in the 'divide and control system'. Lighter *castas* or favoured Africans informed on escape plots or carried out the white man's punishments, but many had little choice except to participate. The truth showed that the enslaved were far from 'gladly and happily served their white masters'. The truth showed that violence and discriminatory racist laws were needed for white people to keep their powers and control. The truth showed that myths, lies and distortions were needed to justify and continue enslavement and colonisation for European greed and power.

What were the white abolition myths?

Spain did not have an abolition crusade similar to Britain because the laws below already existed.

Figure 60: Code Noir of 1742. Nantes history museum

1. **1500s *Sistema de Castas*:** divided into Black, white, and Indian. Racial mixtures resulted in sixteen categories of *castas* that controlled Africans and Indians as inferior. Some mixed-raced people could pass as 'white' and claimed legal freedom if they were white enough.
2. **Manumission and Hiring Out:** Enslaved could buy their freedom, only they were often the poorest people and manumission was expensive. Professor of History, Dr Lyman Johnson's research of manumission records found that, '…slaves' ability to earn and save money was more important than the generosity of the slaveowner in determining access to freedom'.
3. **1785 Code Noir:** Due to fear of slave revolts, restrictive slave code laws were passed. Some were; 30 years of service; survived a middle passage shipwreck; performed a heroic deed, but corrupt officials and greedy slavers meant the enslaved were rarely freed under this code that was adapted from the French.
4. **1789 Slave Code:** provided for 'fair' treatment: no more than 25 whippings; owners must be punished, and the injured set free if they caused 'serious injury, loss of blood, or mutilation'(!); chains or stocks must suit the crime; two hours rest per day and so on. However, there was no enforcement and slavers continued as before.
5. **Military**: free as early as the 1660s but many died and did not experience freedom that they fought for.

These laws only made ENSLAVEMENT MORE MONEY if slaves were treated better!

Professor Emily Berquist believed these reasons 'lessened the need for direct anti-slavery agitation', in contrast to the British abolitionist movement. Paradoxically, Britain had an enthusiastic white abolition movement, even though some of them owned enslaved themselves; owned large plantations and owned slaving vessels. During the 'enlightenment period', abolitionists campaigned because they decided that involvement in slavery degraded them, degraded *white people*. Evidence of chattel enslavement (Brookes ship) was used to gain emotional responses to further their careers. This is called the 'white saviour complex'. The truth is that saving or rescuing Black people is shown clearly today by "charities" or "celebrities" in Africa, objectifying "starving children" to gain donations. In fact, a popular phrase today, to encourage children is, 'Eat your dinner up, there's children starving in Africa!'

***How the blacks has kill'd the whites** in the French Island... a little while ago'*, wrote University historian, Dr James Sidbury. This was an overheard conversation between two enslaved people talking about the Haitian Revolution in Virginia, USA. Victories of Toussaint L'Ouverture and of Dessalines spread as a sign of Black liberty and power. Professor Jeffrey R Kerr-Ritchie believed, 'it is inconceivable that the Haitian Revolution failed to influence scores of slaves'. But not just 'influence'. The truth is that the Haiti Revolution was one of the reasons that eventually led to the abolition of the slave trade. It caused fear amongst the slave holders and ruling classes. But whenever there was a threat to white supremacy, it was subjected to *historia negra negada*. Today, more is known and taught about the French Revolution than the Haiti Revolution.

The Spanish crown forbade any Negroes to be imported from French possessions

The enslaved defeated the most powerful army in the world

In 1804, Haiti was the first Black country in the world to be founded by former slaves.

Three years later, the slave trade was abolished

Figure 61: Burning of the town of Cap-Francais, Saint-Domingue (Haiti), 1795 (colour engraving)

Is the price of manumission freedom?

'Although the enslaved had no civil rights, like children, they had few human rights', claimed Historian, Dr Emily Berquist. In medieval Spanish law, manumission meant release from enslavement. The enslaved could win their freedom by manumission. It was called *Las Siete Partidas* (Seven Part Code) 1567, influenced by Roman law. The truth was that freedom rarely happened. A few laws were:

1. The enslaved was free if he taught the slavers' children.
2. The enslaved was free if married to a free person, with the slavers' permission.
3. The enslaved fought foreign invaders on behalf of Río de la Plata and or Spain, but many did not live to experience the freedom that they fought for.

Historian Dr Lyman Johnson studied 1,482 Buenos Ayres manumission records, dated between 1776 and 1810. He showed that:
- more women than men were manumitted
- more mulattos than West Africans
- more enslaved over 40, or under 15 years old
- 60% were brought by relatives
- 59% of children were manumitted by their families
- more enslaved who were born or inherited in the slavers' household than those who had been purchased.

Figure 62: Black man seeking manumission

It appears therefore, that those who were seen as "non-threatening", gained more manumissions and their freedoms. Under Spanish Law of Coartación, women purchased their freedom by regular payments to their slave owners. Some white slavers recognised children born in their households from enslaved women. These children could be manumitted if baptised and accepted by their slavers. However, gaining manumission was not that straightforward. Professor Peter Blanchard's research found that, 'In 1801, a slave named Cayetana managed to collect the necessary money, but her owner refused to accept it on the grounds that it had been stolen.'

Even if manumission was granted, it was the 'white man's burden' to ensure their good behaviour, or they would be returned to enslavement or criminalised! Today, the United Nations 2019 reported that, 'It is particularly concerned about … persistent structural discrimination against Afro-Argentines, people of African descent and Africans.'

Free or freed or freeborn or free slave?

In 1813, slave trading with Africa was banned throughout Río de la Plata, although enslavement still continued. The Spanish Freedom Womb Act 1813, meant babies born after this date were freeborn, and called *Libertos*. They had to work unpaid for their owners until 16 years old (females) and 20 years old (males), then they were freed. This solved some of the 'white man's burden', many years of forced bondage and enslavement.

Even still, Libertos could be sold and bought after their second birthday. Dr Magdalena Candioti found evidence from 150 Río de la Plata court papers that many enslaved did not know when they were born or how old they were, to get their *Liberto* papers. Slavers also denied *Libertos* freedom by:

Figure 63: Two iron shackles heavily rusted. 1740s.

- changing, hiding, or denying access to birth records and saying Libertos were apprentices
- smuggling those pregnant out of the country, to bring babies back in as enslaved rather than *libertos*' according to George Reid Andrews (1980).

Vagrancy, criminality, or revolution were Spanish fears if freedom was given

The Womb Act meant freedom only if they could pay for it. These captives were freed. The truth is, the Womb Act produced free labour from captive children for years, because white people believed it was their obligation to rule over Black people until they became fully 'civilised'! So babies were not really born free and their mothers were still enslaved. Even if free, they were still seen as 'enslaved' due to skin colour.

Another truth is that being 'freeborn' did not mean a better life. Having been denied any education, good jobs, lack of intergenerational wealth coupled with psychological traumas, some just returned to their original owners when 'freed', and were then known by the strange term of 'free slave'!

Additionally, differences arose between those newly arrived, those born in the Río de la Plata and mixed-raced descendants, those who were free or freed, or freeborn. Some worked hard to assimilate; others remained close with those of similar origin. Others, ashamed of their past, became 'Spaniards', if light enough in skin colour, and did not pass on their heritage. This is the success of the psychological processes contributing towards the myth of, — *aquí no hay negroes*.

What is the myth of the slave house?

A free slave did not live in La Casa del Esclavo Liberto (La Casa Minima - small house) located in San Telmo. But historians disagreed. Some believed that at just two-and-a-half metres wide, it is famous for being the narrowest and only free enslaved house left in the city. Others said that the enslaved were not 'old enough' when the 1813 law came in to be 'freed', because this small house was built in the 1820s.

However, some older Black people were already free or freed before the 1813 Act. And they needed to live somewhere, especially war veterans from the failed British invasions. After all, it was usual for slavers to bury their loyal enslaved near or on their own burial plots. It may have been usual to provide or sub-divide separate areas of slave owners' mansions for the 'free or freed enslaved' to live in.

Figure 64: La Casa Minima (Small House) in San Telmo is the narrowest house in the historic district of San Telmo, Buenos Ayres. The green door with small balcony above extends backwards 13 metres.

In 2016, the Buenos Aires Archaeology Centre found that La Casa Minima was actually the hallway of the larger mansion and that the mansion belonged **'...to a wealthy family with six slaves in 1860...'**. It was sub-divided into smaller units, as was common practice. Today, it has been redeveloped and is one of three larger buildings known as El Zanjón Complex, operating as a History Museum. Underneath lies 2km of underground tunnels for escaping Jesuits, or where the enslaved were kept before dispersion.

San Telmo's barrio of cobbled streets had a strong African presence, as in La Casa Minima, despite the controversy, and is where candombes, murgas (musical theatre), and the tango were born. La Boca in San Telmo is designated of historic and artistic value. Nonetheless, in the nineteenth century, San Telmo became a ghost town due to squalid living conditions and serious yellow fever epidemics. Abandonment saw white European immigrants move in, and then it was redeveloped into touristic *barrio* of today. The stage was set for the misappropriation of culture as part of *historia negra negada*.

Figure 65: Colourful houses in La Boca, near San Telmo where street art and graffiti are active.

Chapter 6 Activities

How did the enslaved resist?
110. Look carefully at the painting. What is it about? Think of another title.
111. What method of resistance are they using?
112. Look at the directions that the man, woman, and child are gazing. Match the words to the direction that you think represents their gazes.
    Past, Present, Future
113. What do you think is happening in the painting? Who are they, what ages, relationships? What is the setting? Where are they going? Where are they coming from? Why? Who helped them? Use your answers to write a paragraph about this painting.

What were the mutiny myths?
114. List the primary and secondary sources on this page. How are these excerpts and images useful for us today?
    a. Change the 'f' into 's' and copy out each excerpt. Whose point of view are these excerpts from?
    b. List 10 or more methods of resistance.
    c. Sort the list into two columns labelled Overt/Covert Actions, and Active/Passive Actions.
    d. Sort the lists into a sliding scale of risk.
    e. Which action would you take? Why? Discuss reasons *not* to resist enslavement.
    f. Which forms of resistance were more effective? Least effective? Why?
    g. What were the consequences of each form of resistance?

What were the white myths of resistance?
115. What are the myths?
116. Why were there numerous reports of 'whippings' or 'manumissions' if the enslaved were 'treated mildly'?
117. What is the white man's burden?
118. Design a poster to show how to behave or treat others with respect today. Label it with words of positive behaviours.
119. If somebody hurt your feelings, how would you respond to make the situation better? Label it with words of positive behaviours.

How the blacks have kill'd the whites….
120. Watch Haitian Revolutions: Crash Course World #30. https://youtu.be/5A_o-nU5s2U 12:34
121. Haiti Slave Revolt 3min History https://youtu.be/1sRE5e2NHDg The slave revolt in Haiti https://www.bbc.co.uk/bitesize/clips/zjgg9j6 1:23
122. Investigate Toussaint L'Overture. BBC Unsung Heroes of Abolition http://www.bbc.co.uk/history/british/abolition/abolitionists_gallery_05.shtml

Is the price of manumission freedom?

123. Explain the following:

   a. the purpose of manumission,
   b. who benefitted the most and why,
   c. the main problem of manumission
   d. whether our meaning of freedom had the same meaning in the 17/18/19th centuries,
   e. what 'future good conduct' means

124. Explain this phrase in one paragraph: ***Freedom Brought Poverty***

125. Why do you think, Cayetana's slaver did not believe her? What, do you think, happened next?

Free or freed or freeborn or free slave?

126. Watch these:

   a. What is a Human right by United Nations? https://youtu.be/JpY9s1Agbsw 1:44
   b. The Covenants by Human Rights Action Center: https://youtu.be/O8kP3pr6XPU 3:32
   c. UN Declaration of Human Rights. https://youtu.be/kJ2XMRJkyv4 3:56
   d. The 30 Articles of Human Rights https://youtu.be/36CUlaqmFi4 2:30
   e. Read more at Equality and Human Rights Commission: https://www.equalityhumanrights.com/en/human-rights/human-rights-act

127. Choose 8 human rights. Rank them from most important to least. Create a poster to promote the most important 4 rights.

128. Look at the shackles photo. Are they a symbol of power for slave owners, or were the enslaved so powerful that they needed to be restrained to protect slave owners? What is your opinion?

What is the myth of the slave house?

129. Take a visual tour of La historia de la Casa Mínima de San Telmo https://youtu.be/NSHajnkkPl8 (in Spanish) 2:55

130. Find out more information about La Casa Minima at El Zanjón Complex here http://www.elzanjon.com.ar/en

131. Many British country houses and mansions were funded by the slave trade. Read Slavery and the British Country house at Historic_England.org: https://historicengland.org.uk/images-books/publications/slavery-and-british-country-house/
Have you visited any?

Chapter 7 Why did the British invade? 61

What is the £20bn bailout to slave-owning Brits? 62

Why is an Argentine an Italian who speaks Spanish and think he's British? 63

Was it conquest of the desert or genocide? 64

In the name of the tourist gaze... 65

Chapter 7 Activities 66

Figure 66: British invasions. Reconquista de Buenos Ayres 1806

Why did the British invade?

Spain joined with France against Britain during the Napoleonic Wars. Britain wanted to get back at Spain, so they invaded Río de la Plata. With the help of the enslaved, the British were defeated twice, known as *Reconquista* and the *Defensa*.

Historian, Dr Seth Meisel pointed out that Governor Jose Maria Paz (1829) replaced a white general with a mulatto named Lorenzo Barcala to persuade thousands free or enslaved to join the military with the promise of freedom. But the truth is that once the war was over, only those who were mutilated and useless were freed.

Figure 67: Portrait of colonel Lorenzo Barcala 1795-1835, for castas. Paz replaced the white master artisan commanding the militia with the mulatto army officer Lorenzo.

Many died on the frontlines for the very freedom that they fought for, not all survivors were freed

1754-1763: The Seven Years' War involved Britain and France fighting over North American colonies. The Treaty of Paris in 1763 ended it. Then Britain fought against France in the Napoleonic Wars, but Spain sided with France, which Britain did not like. Britain borrowed heavily from banks and investors to fund the Seven Years' War. According to the experts, this war caused the French a severe financial disaster that may have sparked the Haiti Revolution, but also Britain's slave trade abolition in subsequent decades.

1806: Britain invaded Buenos Ayres via Río de la Plata. William Beresford and soldiers occupied the city for 46 days before Santiago de Liniers, a French-born Spanish general, drove them out. The British were overwhelmed by a 'rag-tag colonial force' and surrendered according to the 2007 *Guardian News*.

1807: The year that Britain abolished the slave trade, Britain invaded Río de la Plata again! They were defeated a second time, by a Spanish-led army of Indians, Blacks, and Creoles. *'Nothing could be more mortifying than our passage through the streets amidst the rabble who had conquered us. They were very dark-skinned people, short and ill-made, covered with rags, armed with long muskets and some a sword. There was neither order nor uniformity among them'*, said Colonel Lancelot Holland as reported in the *Guardian News*.

1810: Buenos Ayres declared independence from Spain on **May 25, 1810**; celebrated as Venticinco de Mayo. Decades of fighting followed with Brazil, Uruguay and Chile. **1816:** On July 9, 1816, United Provinces of the Río de la Plata was independent from Spain.

What is the £20bn bailout to slave-owning Brits?

On 26 January, 2020, David Jays, a journalist from the UK *Guardian* newspaper reported that, 'In 1833, Britain took out a loan to compensate slavers, only recently paid off.' *The British paid Spain £400,000 in compensation for abolition.*

1813 was not only the Freedom of the Womb Act but the 'Free Soil Act.' Free soil meant freedom if one foot stood on Argentinian soil. However, Dr Emily Berquist's research found '...250 more slave-trade voyages that produced 66,425 slaves ...in 1853'!

In 1816, Argentina gained independence from Spain, and in the 1853 constitution, slavery was declared illegal. However, the truth is that '...slavery in Argentina was never really abolished, it just died of old age', wrote George Reid Andrews (1980). Slave soldiers were no longer needed, and the European wars were vastly expensive. It was not until **1861** that enslavement was officially outlawed in Argentina, with compensation paid to Spanish and other European slavers. No compensation was paid to African nations for the loss of their people and their loss of economic growth and development.

Figure 68: Statue of 'Slavery'. One statue/monument out of three commemorating Black people, in contrast to over 200 for whites in Buenos Ayres

Britain paid Spain to stop enslavement. Nothing at all was paid to the former enslaved who were forbidden an education or to participate in higher skilled trades, or have decent places to live. The truth is that Black descendants went from: **enslaved to free, to second-class citizens, living in poverty...** in the republic that would not have been free from Spain without them. Most free blacks were poorer than the poorest white person.

> *His Britannic Majesty engages to pay, in London, on the 20th of February, 1818, the sum of 400,000 sterling, to such person as his Catholic Majesty shall appoint... Quote 17: Compensation_ Hansard HC Deb 28 January 1818 vol 37 cc67-80*

The reality of abolition was that it was the Black abolitionists, enslaved and free, including the numerous freedom fighters, revolts, mutinies and rebellions that led to the ending of enslavement. Other factors such as the British 'white saviour complex' campaigners; expensive European wars fighting for the 'biggest empire'; rising costs of the European slave trade that helped to demolish enslavement. In any event, the 'white man's burden' was compensated to the amount of £400,000. In today's money that is £20billion!

Why is an Argentine an Italian who speaks Spanish and thinks he's British?

The problem with the 1853 Constitution written by politician Juan Bautista Alberdi, was that it involved 'civilising' Argentina by becoming more like Europe, mainly Britain. It said:

'The Federal Government will encourage European immigration, and it will not restrict...'

Meaning encouraging white European people whilst erasing Black and Indian peoples from the country's history. An exodus of 28,000 whites from the UK, over 2 million Italians, and 1.5 million Spaniards, immigrated to Argentina. The reason given for mass white immigration was to **'improve the species'**, according to the 1853 Constitution.

The humiliating British disasters of 1806 and 1807 led to control by indirect methods, an informal empire. By 1825, both countries signed the Treaty of Friendship, Navigation, and Commerce. The British poured money into Argentina, in return for exports; beef

Figure 69: Western Europe immigration to Argentina

salting plants, agriculture and cattle breeding. At that time, 'Britain was also an especially important market for Argentine meat'. They constructed miles of railways, trams, and stations, vital for moving cattle and beef to the port.

'In the 1850s, thousands of German, French, and Italian colonists settled along the lower Paraná River in Santa Fe province', according to *Encyclopaedia Britannica*. English, Irish, Scottish, and Welsh people immigrated in subsequent decades. Italians had a strong presence in food and street language called "*Lunfardo*" which is mostly, a mixture of African languages with Spanish and Portuguese.

Historian Cyril Hamshere said that 'British in the Argentine were there to make money'. For instance, 'the Liverpool firm that brought an estancia of 72 square leagues and broke it up into sheep farms: in four months a profit of 350% was realised.' Although, the British set a 'bad example for drunkenness (*cliché el borracho inglés*)', claimed Historian David Rock; and Professor Daniel Schavelzon reported criticisms of the railways as 'inefficient and unreliable…'.

The British culture was aspired through English speaking schools, the Torre de los Ingleses (based on London's Big Ben) as a 'gift' to Argentina when Independence was gained; sports (polo and football clubs) and so on. All this led to the 'disappearance' of Black people, lack of intergenerational wealth and *historia negra negada,* from Argentina's nation building and memory.

Was it conquest of the desert or genocide?

In order to 'civilise the nation', as stated in the 1853 Constitution, land outside Buenos Ayres had to be cleared. The Indians had successfully defended the vast Pampas plains and Patagonia for centuries, but were eventually defeated under battles called Desert Campaign, Conquest of the Desert, and the northern Conquest of the Chaco starting from the 1820s, led by President Juan Manuel de Rosas and General Julio Argentino Roca: (Quote 18).

Argentinian anthropologist Dr Carlos Sarasola's research estimated that, 'at least 20,000 Mapuche and other Indians were killed from the Pampas, Patagonia, and Chaco traditional homelands between 1821 and 1899'. Not being white meant being 'inferior, barbaric and uncivilised savages'. Civilising Indians meant naming both Patagonia and Pampas as 'deserts', meaning 'empty'.

Figure 70 Patagonian Indians, Argentina,

> President Julio Argentino Roca said:
> *'Our self-respect as a virile people obliges us to put down as soon as possible, by reason or by force, this handful of savages who destroy our wealth and prevent us from definitely occupying, in the name of law, progress and our own security, the richest and most fertile lands of the Republic.'* Quote 18: 1878 Excerpt from Conquest of the Desert speech

These 'conquests' were said to be civilising missions aimed at Indian criminals who kidnapped women and children. This was just another stereotype of 'kidnapping of white women by native savages', used to justify killing them off the Pampas and Patagonian lands. They were polarised in preparation for extermination. This is similar to what happened to the Black enslaved with official denials, cover-ups and blaming the victims for their 'fate' in subsequent decades.

The truth is, the Pampas and Patagonia had desirable grazing land. After the 'conquests', survivors were forced into 'reservations' or taken prisoners, whilst railroads, *estancias*, sugar mills, new towns and so on were built. And where millions of white Europeans immigrated. However, by 2008, Dr. Amy K. Kaminsky's research found that '...Argentina has a substantial Indian population, numbering about 700,000, though estimates range from 450,000 to 1.5 million.' Today, the president, 'Julio Argentino Roca [is] being removed from banknotes and street names for [his] alleged role in exterminating Indian culture', reported the 2011 *Guardian* newspaper. They concluded that, 'Roca was a genocidal murderer who brought shame to Argentina'.

In the name of the tourist gaze...

Now that the 'desert' had been 'conquered' and the mass of Indian population subjected to extermination, de-Indianisation and land appropriation, Britain and other European nations became wealthy by building *estancias*, factories, and railways, using Indian survivors as cheap labour. One of these railways was the *La Trochita Patagonia Express,* built in the coldest part of Argentina, Patagonia.

The 'Old Patagonia Express' is a narrow-gauge steam railway. Since 1999, it has been a National Historic Monument. The train rides through two of the most beautiful national parks in Patagonia: the *Nahuel Huapi National Park* and *Los Alerces National Park*. Today, it works as a heritage railway.

Figure 71: The Old Patagonian Express

Survivors still live in the area and are direct descendants of the Mapuche peoples. Every March, a religious Mapuche speaking ceremony takes place in Camaruco. However, lifestyles have been further eroded or adapted for the tourist gaze, in the form of 'authentic traditional entertainment' at some train stations where they perform for the tourists. Nonetheless, they have always been active in fighting for their own freedom and as a result temporary Laws were passed in 2006, extended in 2009 and 2013, to survey their territories aimed at stopping land grabs by industries. But the descendants are fighting to make these temporary laws permanent.

Figure 72: Tren a las nubes crossing viaduct by Casa Rosada

The Tren a las Nubes (Train of the clouds) is in the Salta province, where Quechua-speaking Black descendants live. Salta has the fifth highest railway train in the world with an altitude of 4200 meters. La Polvorilla Viaduct is the highest point of the train at 4,220 meters above sea level. It is a curved bridge, 220 meters long, and measures 64 meters (210ft.) tall, according to *Encyclopaedia Britannica*. Original peoples and their Creole-assimilated descendants built these structures under terrible conditions, and many died forgotten.

Chapter 7 Activities

Why did the British invade?
132. Did Britain have the right to interfere? Why, Why not?
133. Click and read about Black Argentina Army Heroes. Scroll down to No. 7 for Colonel Lorenzo Barcala https://afroestilo.com/2014/05/08/heroes-afrodescendientes-argentinos-invisibilizados/ and https://en.wikipedia.org/wiki/Lorenzo_Barcala
134. Design a poster about Colonel Lorenzo Barcala, include a brief biography.

What is the 20bn bailout to slave-owning Brits?
135. Why was enslavement abolished? Give 3 reasons each from the slavers point of view and then 3 from the enslaved point of view.
136. Read 'Top British firms to pay compensation over founders slavery links.' www.telegraph.co.uk/news/2020/06/17/companies-britain-linked-slave-trade-say-today/ What is your opinion of the compensation?
137. Watch ARGENTINA/ AFRO-ARGENTINIANS @ https://youtu.be/a_P4STigGco 2:43
138. What do you think of the statue when you look at it? Does it represent 'the enslaved'? Design your own statue to represent 'The Captive'.

Why is an Argentine an Italian who speaks Spanish and thinks he's British?
139. What is immigration? Why was European immigration encouraged?
140. Read the USA Constitution https://constitutionus.com/ What are the first 3 words? Why are those words important?
141. Read the 13th Amendment in the USA Constitution. What did this amendment make illegal in the United States?
142. The UK has never had a formal constitution. Make up your own model constitution that lists ten rights that you think all people should have.
143. How can you create rights that don't make other people's lives more difficult?

Was it conquest of the desert or genocide?
144. How many Conquests took place? Why did these 'Conquests' happen? Give 3 or more reasons.
145. Produce art work or a poem in memory of the Indian victims.
146. Read the 1853 Constitution at https://www.constituteproject.org/constitution/Argentina_1994?lang=en

    a. Debate the 'conquests' and enslavement in terms of Articles 15, 16, and 25 of the 1853 Constitution.
    b. Why did enslavement continue for decades after the law banning enslavement?

In the name of the tourist gaze…
147. Watch Argentina 2014, The Trochita is back https://youtu.be/WLj6t_p3zvQ 14.57

    a. How many different steam trains are on this line?
    b. What is a freight train? What is a tourist train?

148. Watch Civil Engineering Crash Course- How to build bridges and buildings: https://youtu.be/-xbtnz4wdaA?t=256 8:45
149. Watch How do Steam Engines Work? https://youtu.be/xnClSss50pI 9:35 Draw a diagram to show how steam can have enough force to move an entire locomotive and carriages.

Chapter 8

Why is Argentina known as the whitest nation? 68

What was the blanqueamiento of Black People? 69

Why was the Black Mother of Argentina forgotten? 70

How were the enslaved rescued? 71

Who was the real El Negro Falucho? 72

Chapter 8 Activities 73

Figure 73: Slavery in 1529

Why is Argentina known as the whitest nation?

Argentina is the only South American nation that has tried to erase the *mestizos*, *mulattoes*, Indians and Africans from its history. Explorer, Samuel Haigh reported in 1817, that there were '...few "pure whites" in Buenos Aires and most people were of mixed ancestry or black'. Historian Professor George Reid Andrews calculated in 1838 that, '... there were 15,000 Black people according to the national census'. But 'By 1887 only 8,000 were recorded ...'. By the late nineteenth century, Black people had supposedly 'disappeared', — *Aquí no hay negroes* is another popular phrase.

Professor Miriam Gomes, from the University of Buenos Aires, said, 'Historians are somewhat to blame for the stereotypes of South America's "whitest" nation.' Eurocentric historians believed that the sudden mass disappearance of Black people was due to:

- the forced military service in the brutal independent wars
- mass immigration of white European men that outnumbered Black men
- less Black men meant Black women had white partners
- several serious epidemics of yellow fever in the tenements of San Telmo

Yet, the truth is that Black people did not disappear. They ceased to exist as a forgotten part of 'modernising' Argentina. A European white history meant distorting reality, inventing lies and myths to create a sanitised and whitewashed version without Indians and Black peoples' contributions. Eurocentric historians and officials rewrote history, only to suit white people which was then taught to both Black and white children for generations and still is, to some extent.

Figure 74: Argentina's Black population has been systematically erased.

Being invisible meant exclusion from white society and a denial that racism ever existed. Being invisible meant white people did not have to deal with the racism that excluded Black people from its history and conscience; despite the significant contributions to the urban and rural economies they made. Being invisible meant white people did not have to deal with Black people living in poverty from one generation to the next. A United Nations Human Rights fact-finding mission in March 2019 concluded that, 'Exclusion has been for so long that they [people of African descent] need support from international organisations'.

What is the blanqueamiento of Black people?

Whitening. Argentines, today believe that they were not involved in the slave trade and that Black people have disappeared. Both are wrong. The truth is, Black people were 'lightened' by the seventeenth century; 'blanqueamiento' by the eighteenth; and 'sanitised' by the nineteenth.

Today's racial and cultural silence is so deep that racism is excused and normal that the belief of, *aquí no hay negroes*, prevails throughout Argentinian society. Historian Professor George Reid Andrew, said that, 'By 1800, 30 percent of the inhabitants of Buenos Ayres were of African ancestry, the large majority of whom had been born in Africa and were identified as Black in official documents.' How then, did Black people supposedly 'vanish'?

Figure 75: BBC Video: What it's like to be Black and Argentine. See Activities

- *Mestizo* people denied their African ancestry to avoid the stigma and embarrassment of their heritage, – *blanqueamiento (whitening) process*
- Manumission officials used contradictory terms such as 'white mulatto' on documents, – *blanqueamiento process*
- Census-takers labelled *Mestizos* as white; Mestizo population then became the *Castizo* population, – *blanqueamiento process*
- White growth rate exceeded the Black growth due to mass white immigration, – *blanqueamiento process*
- Mass imprisonment for minor or fabricated crimes. Little has changed. Black people are still more likely to be imprisoned or killed by law enforcement and receive harsher penalties and longer sentences than white people as a percentage of the population. The United Nations 2019 noted that the, '...disproportionate use of [police] force against people of African descent can turn to deadly violence', – *disappearance process*
- Since 1855, the census included 'no information on race in its questionnaire', said Reid Andrews (1980), – *disappearance process*
- Decrease in new arrivals when the slave trade was abolished and aging of current enslaved or free, – *disappearance process*
- Mothers had less children or avoided having any due to enslaved status; also subjected to the worst healthcare, – *disappearance process*

The truth is that Black people had not disappeared at all. It was a deliberate effort to remove Black people from official documents so Argentinian politicians could pretend that they have 'modernised the species' and produced a 'regeneration of the races'. Furthermore, Argentina is immense and not all Black people live in Buenos Aires. However, '...for the first time in over 100 years, there was a question about African ancestry', [on the census] wrote African Argentine University historian Erika Edwards. Her investigations of the 2010 census revealed that in the Córdoba province, '**62,642** people had one or more African ancestor'. She said that, 'Though many have white skin, their veins flow of Black blood'.

Why was the Black Mother of Argentina forgotten?

Figure 76: Image of Maria Remedios Del Valle from Televisión Pública Argentina

María Remedios Del Valle was born on 8 November 1766 and died in 1847. She was the daughter of the person who enslaved her. Maria left the house when she found this out. Known as Madre de la Patria, the Mother of Argentina in English, because of her war efforts but recognition was not always the case. She was erased from national memory due to deliberate, personal and structural discrimination because, *aquí no hay negroes!*

María was a revolutionary woman who took part in many battles. General Manuel Belgrano was a military leader and women were not allowed in his army. He said '… real women mothers had the mission to procreate and raise virtuous, brave, patriotic citizens, ready to fight…'. Maria ignored the General's attitude and took part with her two daughters, known as the "Girls from Ayohúma", and her husband. She was shot several times; taken prisoner; whipped for six or nine days; her family were killed, but she escaped, and then helped others to escape. María continued to fight in the wars.

> *…scorching heat, thirst, wounded and disorder, together with the image of three "dark" or "brown" women [mother and two daughters] who, in an act of unforgettable courage, quenched thirst and healed to the sick.*
>
> Quote 19: Military officer, Gregorio Aráoz de Lamadrid in Florencia Guzmán (2016) study.

After the wars of independence, María survived by begging on the streets near the Recova, until she gained a small war pension. By 1836, she was renamed 'Doña Remedios Rosas: The Head Cavalry Sergeant'. Still, she died poor and forgotten, with only the battle scars that she was proud of, according to the experts. In the late nineteenth century, Argentina wanted to have a white history, and erased or culturally misappropriated any memories or achievements or involvement of Black people in the nation-building of Argentina.

In 2013, efforts by African Argentines resulted in 8 November as National Day of African Culture. However, in 2019, the United Nations urged that '… the government must promote a nationwide public dialogue on the significance of the history of African Argentines, including their current human rights situation.' By late 2020, following the United Nations recommendations, the Ministry of Culture launched a national competition with substantial prizes, to remember María in sculpture, poetry, popular music, art, documentary and cartoon. The Ministry's reasons are '… to promote public policies with a decolonial, anti-patriarchal, anti-racist and reparative perspective of the systematic absence and invisibility to which Afro-Argentines, Afro-descendants and or Africans have been subjected'.

How were the enslaved rescued?

> Article. 1/E; Decreto de 31 de Mayo del presente año para el rescate de Esclavos se hace extensive á toda la Provincia de Buenos-Ayres.
> Quote 20: Extract from Black Troops Regiment of Freemen Decree - 1812-1818

The 1813 Free Womb Decree not only freed those born after 1813 or those who stood on Argentina soil for the first time, but the forced enslavement into the military or else, imprisonment. It was called the Rescate de Escalvos, meaning 'slave rescue' (Quote 20). 'Most were donated by their owners or sold into the military', wrote Professor Peter Blanchard. Propaganda encouraged ideas of the military spirit as freeing the enslaved from enslavement, whilst being a soldier that freed Río de la Plata from Spain.

The 1813 Act forced free men into the Regiment of Libertos. By 1816, the country was independent from Spain. In 1829, the enslaved used their position in the military to fight for their educational rights. Historian, Dr Seth Meisel said that Governor Jose Maria Paz from the Córdoba province agreed because he needed the enslaved to fight. The Governor said '…it was inconsistent that *castas* serve in the militia and yet be denied entrance into public schools.' However, when allowed in schools, the truth is, Black children were subjected to racial segregation and taught to despise their blackness.

> [t]he officers of the Battalions of Pardos and Morenos will be treated with esteem, no one will be permitted to insult them in words or deeds, and among those of their respective classes they will be distinguished and respected. Quote 21: Felix Colon de Larraitegui's legal handbook, (1778)

An earlier unit named *Pardos y Morenos* Regiment meaning The Mixed Race and Black Regiment (*Pardoes* - light skin and *Morenos* - dark skin) was formed but exposed to discriminatory military practices. Felix Colon, a General Lieutenant for Spain, ruled that the *Pardoes y Morenos* Regiment must be treated with respect (Quote 21).

'The long and bitter warfare between 1810 and 1826 helped to undermine the institution that kept the enslaved in chains', according to Professor Peter Blanchard. Most enslaved between 12 and 50 years old became 'slave soldiers', or 'slaves in arms', and 'ex-slaves became citizens' by fighting wars, as historians have described. Professor Blanchard said that 'many thousands of captives joined up to escape from the harshness of slave life, to show that they were not property, and to challenge the 'happy slave' stereotype'.

Of course, the truth is that many enslaved were not 'rescued' at all. Few gained their freedom after the wars; many died on the frontlines to free Río de la Plata from Spain, and many were mutilated. It was not white moral outrage that ended enslavement, but the nation fighting for its own freedom which ultimately ended up freeing the captives as well, according to the experts. Nonetheless, those descendants of the Black captives who fought for Río de la Plata so that the porteños could rule themselves, were erased as *historia negra negada* or subjected to the heroic stereotypes of *El Negro Falucho*.

Who was the real El Negro Falucho?

Born in Buenos Ayres, Antonio Ruiz or Ruizan fought in the military for over fourteen years. He was a dedicated soldier who refused to betray his country. Antonio was shot dead by the Spanish in 1824 for refusing to honour the enemy flag at a guard post. He died shouting, 'Long live Buenos Ayres!'

Bartolomé Mitre was Argentine President between 1862 to 1868. He led military campaigns and wrote about Antonio Ruiz's bravery in 1857. However, later historians doubted his written account, said it was a '...Bartolomé Mitre's creation', even though the President took evidence and personal testimonies from Ruiz's commanding officers at that time. Historians disagreed because:

- *Falucho* was a general nickname for unknown Black heroes;
- The book *'Los Negroes Argentinos'* by Manuel J. Mantilla in 1899, had two *Faluchos; one in* the 8th Battalion of the Andes Army and the other a corporal in 1819;

Figure 77: Monument to a Black soldier Antonio Ruiz or 'El Negro Falucho. Located in the Palmero barrio in 1897

He was free and a citizen as soon as he donned the martial jacket'
Quote 22: From Los Negroes Argentinos by Manuel J Mantilla 1889

However, despite the land being drenched with the blood of Black men defending national freedom from foreign invaders and being forced into the military, this is another example of '...not giving importance to the person because of his race', wrote Dr. Donald S. Castro. Yet, historians agreed that 'a black soldier died courageously ... while refusing to honour the Spanish royal flag', but his name is disputed and therefore nicknamed *El Falucho*.

Slave soldiers fed into another popular stereotype as the best soldiers. They were hardier, braver, self-sacrificing heroes who gave their lives to forge a nation for their white slavers! This is despite the fact that many were forced into the military with discriminating pay and treatment. Rather than uncovering how Black people were sold into the military; rather than uncovering the discrimination suffered; rather than uncovering Black people who rose to be high level officers under difficult circumstances, eurocentric historians perpetrate the semi-mythological hero status of Black soldiers, as saviours of white people, and as unnamed disputed *Negroes Faluchos*.

Chapter 8 Activities

Why is Argentina known as the whitest nation?
150. What is a Census? Research UK Census and find out four interesting facts about the UK.
     https://www.ons.gov.uk/peoplepopulationandcommunity
151. How did Black people disappear from the Argentina's census?
152. Why would Argentina's government want Black people to disappear?

What was the blanqueamiento of Black People?
153. Watch the video from the BBC. What its like to be Black and Argentine. Then answer the questions about the video:
     https://www.bbc.co.uk/news/av/world-latin-america-46641620/what-it-s-like-to-be-black-and-argentine

     a. How many centuries ago was Argentina one-third Black?
     b. Why is Jesica Salinas Lamadrid angry? What do people think of Jesica?
     c. What European countries do people think Argentines are descended from?
     d. Give three reasons why people think Blacks may have vanished?
     e. What does genocide mean?
     f. What is systematic racism? Clue: Who or what may have the answer to the death of Angel Acosta Martinez 's brother?
     g. How long has Angel Acosta Martinez 's brother been waiting?

Why was the Black Mother of Argentina forgotten?
154. What qualities and values make a hero? Is Maria a hero? Why/Why not?
155. Read more about Maria and the competitions at the National Museum and Ministry of Culture:

     a https://cabildonacional.cultura.gob.ar/noticia/maria-remedios-del-valle-la-madre-de-la-patria/
     b. https://www.cultura.gob.ar/maria-remedios-del-valle-valiente-capitana-9620/ Which medium will you use?
     c. Design your own sculpture, poetry, popular music, art, documentary or cartoon in her memory.

How were the enslaved rescued?
156. Find out some facts about the Rescate de Escalvos (slave rescue).
157. Find out the dates of the Wars of Independence and other wars that took place.
158. What were the uniforms of the soldiers like? Do some research and draw them.

Who was the real El Negro Falucho?
159. Give examples to show the meaning of these words: **patriotic, heroic, mythical**
160. What evidence is there to show that Antonio existed?
161. Why are Black enslaved soldiers called El Negro Falucho?

Chapter 9

What is the Candombe dance?	75
How and why did tango change colour?	76
Who were the payadores and what are pulperias?	77
From slave food to national dish….	78
How to serve the drink of the gods	79
Chapter 9 Activities	80

Figure 78: Candombé, impressionist painting by Pedro Figari.

What is the Candombe dance?

'In the 1830s, free blacks and slaves were arrested if the police found them at racially mixed dance gatherings without a license...', according to Dr Alex Borucki. Instead, people met in their houses according to origin or nation. Religious meetings, manumissions and candombes were discussed in places such as *La Capilla de los Negroes*, Black Chapel in English. Built in the 1860s and located in east Buenos Ayres, it is a UNESCO Historic Site since 1962.

Eurocentric historians believed that Black people had no culture because they were seen as passive victims. This is another myth. In 1951, an African American anthropologist, Irene Diggs said that, 'When freedom proved impossible, people attempted to make their lives worth living under the most appalling conditions.' She recognised that: 'He has danced to relieve himself of desperation; sung to keep from crying; danced to keep from rebelling; and sung to make the heavy work lighter.' The Codes of 1789 regulated the 'recreation' of slaves, but singing and dancing could not be stopped and cost the captives practically nothing.

Figure 79: A depiction from 1870 of Afro-Uruguayan dancers and musicians performing candombe in Montevideo, Note facial expressions.

The candombe dance is both a creation of a new culture whilst at the same time using African traditions, such as the drumming and the thumb piano. Experts agreed that candombe means 'relating to Blacks' in the Kikongo language. Kikongo is one language of the Bantu-speakers from the Kongo Kingdom. In 1969, historian and musicologist, Nestor Ortiz Oderigo's research showed that, 'Candombe derived from a Bantu language spoken in the Kongo and in Angola, which means 'black' or 'belonging to black culture'. Described as:

- using 'the typical African "call and response" pattern as part of the lyrics'
- the dancing in a circle, individuals or group, without upright postures
- spontaneous wild dancing and rhythms with jolting, lively movements

Milonga is a drum-based dance. It started where there was not much room in their houses and close partner dancing evolved. White people saw this as obscene and corrupt. Still, people would say that they were going to a 'milonga'. That was the same as going to 'tango parties'. Milonga was also linked with the guitars of the payadores, – the entertainers of the gaucho world of the Pampas. Eventually, the milonga and candombe combined to create the tango.

How and why did tango change colour?

Tango started out in the overcrowded tenements of La Boca in the former enslaved *barrio* of San Telmo, Buenos Ayres. In 1969, musicologist Ortiz Oderigo's research concluded that, 'early tango was mostly for men ... prevalent throughout both Sudanic and Bantu [speakers] areas'.

The tango was a mixture of the jolting, lively movements of the candombe, with the steps and close-up dancing of the milonga, but sanitised to remove any African references. Upright, stiff postures replaced the wild energetic movements; paired dancing, instead of groups or individuals; slower music; jerky-type steps instead of jerky bodies. In UNESCO's 1977 Latin America research, they found:

- 'Tango is a corruption of the name "Shango", the Nigerian god of storms and thunder'
- the 'Bantu word "tamgu", means "to dance"
- 'Tango is a Kongolese word Iango' which is a type of dance
- 'Tango is of pure African origin', according to Dr. Matthew Karush's 2012 research
- 'Tango is found as a place-name today in Angola and Mali', wrote Dr Sarah Quesda in 2015, 'developed in Spain and brought to Americas by the enslaved'
  - According to History Professor Simon Collier, 'tango is almost certainly either of direct African provenance', or 'may come from the 'Portuguese "tangere", meaning to touch... assimilated by African enslaved from their captors'
  - Uruguayan singer and composer, Alfredo Zitarrosa (in UNESCO), explained the progression as, '**The milonga is the daughter of the candombe, as the tango is the son of the milonga**'.

Figure 80: Couple dancing Argentine tango

The famous tango came from African roots

However, there is little memory of Tango's origins in popular culture, because it has been misappropriated, whitened and sanitised for and by the mass of European immigrants and media during the late nineteenth century. **'From the enslaved, tango passed to the poor, from them to the middle class, to the aristocracy and then worldwide',** according to UNESCO. In 2009, tango has been listed as Intangible Cultural Heritage, and African roots have been recognised by some experts, although this is not widely known. Contributing to the myth of, – *aquí no hay negroes*, because Black people have supposedly 'disappeared' and therefore subjected to *historia negra negada*.

Who were the payadores and what are pulperias?

Whilst simultaneously admiring and mocking Black music, racism led to hundreds of white men blacking their faces and performing 'white imitation of black dances'. They called themselves Black names such as, '*Los Negros Esclavo, Los Negros Candomberos* or *La Perla Africana*', wrote Dr Matthew Karush, (The Negro Slaves, The Black Candombes or The African Pearl in English).

Gabino Ezeiza, the son of an ex-slave, was a Black gaucho, a recognised talented payador and 'A noted Black gaucho singer storyteller', said Historian Dr Donald S. Castro. One of Gabino's popular storyteller songs paid tribute to the memory of "El Negro Falucho". Born in 1858 in the drum and tango *barrio* of San Telmo, he was the most famous payador. There is '**...**a dilapidated bust of Gabino Ezeiza, its nameplate missing, set in a small playground ... ...in his memory as a payador', said Reid Andrews.

Figure 81: Pulperías, said to be low-class places where people (mainly gauchos) of various origins met to drink, sing, gamble and gossip

'Some Black people were payadores and owned "bars" called *Pulperias* where they retold stories with music', wrote Dr Alex Borucki (2018). 'Payadores try to outdo each other with improvised rhyming verses and riddles, an early form of sophisticated insults to opponents', [rapping poetry with guitars]. Dr Borucki said that 'Two enslaved operated a *pulpería* in San Isidro during the mid-1780s, known as the *Pulpería de los Negritos*. It was a popular meeting place for gossip, gambling, drinking and singing'.

Figure 82: Gabino Ezeiza-A Payador, Famous Payador Singer Pic: José Maria Oteroz

Historians recognised that the first tango music was composed by Gabino Ezeiza. However, 'Most black payadores were remembered without a name, and recalled only as, 'un negro payador', said Dr Castro. Argentine Professor Dr Anahi Viladrich concluded that, 'the Afro-Argentines who had contributed to the musical creation of the creole tango, were ultimately removed from the genre they had helped craft.' Still, Gabino Ezeiza was already established as a rural gaucho payador before the elite porteños could "whiten" him. Now, every 23 of July is celebrated as 'Payador's Day' in memory of Gabino Ezeiza. The day that he "won" his payador singing duel with a white opponent in 1884.

From slave food to national dishes...

'Fifty beasts, introduced by Juan de Garay in 1580', according to historian A. L. Lloyd (1951), turned into, '...600,000 a year by the nineteenth century'. Many gauchos, enslaved and free, worked in the *mataderos* (slaughterhouses) and meat factories butchering cattle. It is unsurprising that Argentines now eat vast quantities of beef. Traditional gaucho food is "*asado*", that is piles of barbequed cuts of beef, now a popularised weekly tradition.

Figure 83: Los Chinchulines

'African Argentines also gave Argentina its favourite dish, called *Chinchulines*', said historian George Reid Andrew. 'These are braided and barbecued cow intestines.' *Chinchulines* are served in a mixed grill called "*Parrillada*". Chinchulines or Chitterlings (US), started out in the mataderos as food for the poor, where the gauchos processed the cattle.

> Two Negro women were dragging along the entrails of an animal. A mulatta woman carrying a heap of entrails slipped in a pool of blood and fell lengthwise under her coveted booty...Four hundred Negro women unwound heaps of intestines in their laps, picking off one by one those bits of fat which the butcher's avaricious knife had overlooked.
> Quote 23: El Matadero (The Slaughterhouse) by Esteban Echeverria (1809) quoted in Angle Flores (1942) New Mexico quarterly

Dr Andrew Sluyter described the *mataderos* as, '...the hundred or so head to be salted that day lay dead, and the gauchos proceeded to dress them, a spectacle of eight to ten men dripping with blood, knives in hand...'. He described Charles Darwin's reaction when he visited Buenos Ayres in 1833 as: '*horrible and revolting; the ground almost made of bones; and the horses, and riders are drenched with gore*'.

Figure 84: Engraving of the inside of a Saladero at Fray Bentos in 1880 Chapel Hill Libraries.

Argentine Esteban Echevarria's infamous fictional novel, *El Abattoir*, described Black women fighting with the dogs for the intestines that the gauchos threw out for the vultures. Such imagery ensured that the racist symbol of Black people with dogs remained in the national memory. Yet today, '*El Abattoir*' is one of the most studied texts in Latin American literature', according to Norman Giovanni, translator for *El Abattoir* (1871).

How to serve the drink of the Gods

Yerba maté (mah-tay) said to be the 'drink of the gods,' or 'a holy drink' and a 'national gaucho tradition'. The *Ilex paraguariensis* holly tree provides the leaves for the drink. Although it started in Paraguay, Argentina is the world's largest producer.

The Tupi-Guarani speakers were the first users of the plant. They believed that it healed the sick, extended life and increased energy. According to the scientists, it has many vitamins, minerals and healing benefits. The explorer, 'Juan de Solís reported that the Guarani Indians ... brewed a leaf tea that "produced exhilaration and relief from fatigue", wrote History Professor Dr Adalberto López.

The yerba, (herb) is chewed or drunk in a maté, (cup) from a bombilla, (straw). At the end of the bombilla is a strainer. These items are made from wood or metal and are popular tourist souvenirs today.

Figure 85: TOMADO MATE (taking maté): Africans were essential to the region's production of foodstuffs; defence and animal husbandry.

The sixteenth century Jesuits in the *Reducciones* sent Indians into the forests for yerba, but many died during the long journey into the forest wetlands. Then the Jesuits grew yerba in the *Missions* until they were expelled and took their knowledge with them. The drink was rediscovered decades later but it did not become as popular as tea or coffee.

In the cities, wealthy porteños' matés and bombillas were made from gold and silver and it was the enslaved Black girls' job was to prepare and serve it properly. On the Pampas, the gauchos drink yerba maté before the day starts, with friends, and to welcome strangers. This ancient custom has now become authenticated by elite porteños and tourists romanticising about a traditional past. Some Indians say yerba maté has been culturally misappropriated by the US trendy drinks market, who sell it as a new-found miracle plant, even though it has been around for centuries. Today, every November 30 is National Maté Day which celebrates the date of the first Indian Argentine Governor, Andrés Guacurarí (1778 -1825) of the Corrientes province.

Chapter 9 Activities

What is the Candombe dance?

162. Watch these:

- a. Candombe Milonga performed by Central Ave Dance Ensemble https://youtu.be/Ck8nfkv5l0Y 6:19
- b. 2010 STF Grand Milonga 09 - Francisco Forquera y Carolina Bonaventura Milonga dance finals https://youtu.be/1VRj8m84Qls 3:46
- c. List the differences between the two dances in a Venn diagram. Which dance do you prefer, and why?

163. Find out more about the artist Pedro Figari and Candombe at http://www.candombe.com/english.html

How and why did tango change colour?

164. Watch these:

- a. Guillermina y Gustavo. Tango Negro Tango dancers https://youtu.be/ulaOHr7Iha8 2:24
- b. 2010 STF Grand Milonga 09 - Francisco Forquera y Carolina Bonaventura Milonga dance finals https://youtu.be/1VRj8m84Qls
- c. List the differences between the candombe, milonga, and tango, in a Venn diagram. Which dance do you prefer, and why?
- d. Which of these musical genres have African roots? hip-hop, reggae, jazz, salsa, disco, rock, rumba…

Who were the payadores and what are pulperias?

165. Explain the meaning of pulperia and payador. Give examples.

166. Research facts about payador Carlos Posadas at To Do Tango https://www.todotango.com/creadores/biografia/852/Carlos-Posadas/

167. Listen to his music. Un Reculié - Carlos Posadas (Tango Argentino 1900-1930) https://youtu.be/Tt5sikqpMu4 2:10

- a. Listen to Juan Carlos Caceres - 02. Tango Negro, with lyrics in Spanish. https://youtu.be/9uQh5RfE2XA 3:45
- b. Can you identify the African words in the lyrics?

From slave food to national dish…

168. What are the health risks eating a little or a lot of beef?

169. Argentine Esteban Echeverría wrote El Abattoir. What impression do you think, white people would have when reading this book?

170. Watch video Chinchulines Trenzado https://youtu.be/0CWMRppR_C4 2:54. Make Chinchulines or find some in shops. How tasty are they?

How to serve the drink of the Gods

171. Read What is Yerba Maté: Uses, Benefits and Brands https://teaallure.com/what-is-yerba-mate/ to find out more about Yerba Maté

172. Watch, The Dark History Behind Yerba Maté https://youtu.be/v98C9ieKmAU 2:11

173. Research information about the Indian Argentine governor, Andrés Guacurarí and create a biography. Include a painting or sketch of the Governor, different spellings of his name, his military career, location of the province. Add some personal information as well.

Figure 86: 1841. The Governor of Buenos Ayres granting freedom to the enslaved. Juan Manuel de Rosas was a dictator backed by state terrorism from 1829-1852. He was exiled in 1852 to Britain, where he died in 1877.

United Nations Human Rights	**82**
Glossary	**83**
References 1, 2, 3, 4	**84, 85, 86, 87**
Picture and Quote Credits	**88**
Index	**89**
Author	**90**

United Nations Human Rights: Argentina Reports

In 2017, the United Nations International Convention reported on the Elimination of All Forms of Racial Discrimination in Argentina. (CERD/C/ARG/CO/21-23). From their fact-finding mission, amongst other recommendations, the Argentina government is urged to:

1. 'Adopt a comprehensive policy to combat racism and racial discrimination'
2. 'Combat racist hate speech.'
3. '…ensure that indigenous peoples are protected from forced evictions.'
4. '…implement a suitable programme of measures and policies for International Decade for People of African Descent.'
5. '…prevention of racial discrimination … [in] the criminal justice system.'

In 2018, a further report (E/C.12/ARG/CO/4) stated:
6. The 2020 census, should include questions to '… identify indigenous peoples, persons of African descent…'
7. As in 2017, they must '… implement the International Decade for People of African descent 2015-2024.'
8. '… increased visibility should ensure that Afro-Argentines benefit from development programmes aimed at improving their life quality and the enjoyment of human rights.'

In 2019, the United Nations Working Group of Experts on People of African Descent stated:
9. '…combat all forms of racism, racial discrimination, xenophobia, Afrophobia and related intolerance.'
10. '… particularly concerned about the long-standing invisibility and the persistent structural discrimination against Afro-Argentines, people of African descent and Africans.
11. '…include in the curricula the history of the trade in enslaved Africans, … history and contributions of people of African descent in Argentina.'
12. '…reduce the inequality gaps that affect the Afro-descendant and African population, a product of the structural racism resulting from the colonization process and the slave trade.'

Read the full reports at: https://www.ohchr.org/EN/NewsEvents/Pages/DisplayNews.aspx?NewsID=24350&LangID=E

GLOSSARY

Abolition: official ending of the slave trade

Anthropologist: a person who studies the science of human beings and their cultures

Archaeologist: a person who studies the science of objects that people have left behind

Assiento: a contract to buy slaves for Spain

Assimilation: become like others in a different group

Auction: sell to someone with the most money

Balde sin fondo: bottomless bucket that the Senegambians may have adapted to the Pampas

Barrio: neighbourhood

Blanqmamiento: whitening of Black people

Boleradoras: a throwing weapon used by gauchos

Bombilla: metal straw with filter for drinking mate

Candombe: music and dance that originated in the Río de la Plata, with African roots

Chattel slavery: own and treat people, their children and children's children as their own property – created by white Europeans

Colony: a country controlled by another more powerful country. Spain controlled Rio de la Plata

Conquistador: a 15th to 17th century explorer and conqueror for the Iberian Peninsula

Constitution: laws by which a country is governed

Criollo: Argentine born, of Spanish descent

Decree: a rule of law

Discrimination: unfairly treating people because of their race or colour in organisations or socially

Economic historian: a person who studies how money was used in a country in the past

Encomienda: a Spanish legal system that forced Indians to work and pay them money

Enslaved: a slave, of being controlled and dominated and without freedom

Eurocentric: white point of view that ignores, distorts, lies about aspects of history such as culture, ethnicity, race and people; also spreads lies as facts

European slave trade: three routes form a triangle between Africa, Europe, and Americas in the buying and selling of goods and Africans. Also called triangular or transatlantic slave trade

Enslavement: being controlled, dominated or forced to work for another without payment

Fallacy: an argument which claims to be factual while in reality it is not.

Gaucho: an Argentinian cowboy on the Pampas

Genocide: to deliberately kill a group of people because of their race, ethnicity, or religion

Geologist: a person who studies rocks scientifically to find out how the Earth changes over time

Gracias al Sacar: buying a certificate that converts mixed-race people to white people

Historian: a person who studies the passing of time and the events that happen within that time

Illusion: seeing or hearing something and believing it as a fact when it is not true – similar to a trick

Indentured servant: a contract of their own free will to work for a set number of years in exchange for something, such as accommodation costs

Indian peoples: people who lived in the country before the invaders – also called indigenous, native or original peoples

Institutionalised or systemic racism: invisible systems of white privileges inherited by organisations such as law and justice, schools and education, health and medicine, housing and land, finance and money, occupations and professions

Liberto: children born after 1813 were free after many years of bondage

Manumission: legally buying own freedom

Mate: a gourd for drinking yerba herbs

Middle passage: crossing the Atlantic Ocean to and from West Central Africa and the Americas on slaving ships in horrific conditions

Milonga: faster version of the tango; African roots

Misappropriate: dominate groups who take, steal, or use part of another culture as their own without acknowledgement; usually from less dominant groups

Myth: an old story that has been around so long that most people believe it but existing only in their imagination

Negro: derogatory name for Black people, used in the past

Pampas: a vast flat grassland, mostly treeless area

Patagonia: vast region in the far south of Argentina

Payador: a singer who plays the guitar with improvised lyrics, against another rival payador

Peon: unskilled, menial agricultural work

Pieza de indias: a unit of measurement

Plantation: a large farm growing one crop

Prejudice: negative judgement about a group without knowledge about the group

Propaganda: misleading information from officials – often hard to tell if it is true or false

Pulperia: a pub, country store where payadores sing

Racism: system of advantage for whites

Racist: a person who believes he or she is better and superior to other races, based on skin colour

Resistance: refuse to obey orders

Rebellion or insurrection: people who openly fight against laws, and are usually armed

Revolution: To turn a nation upside down and replace the ruler

Sistema de Castas: a Spanish system of Black, White, Indian relationships and their mixed-race children

Stereotype: a negative attitude about one group of people, based on how they look from the outside

Tango: a gathering to dance; tango music; a partner dance; from African roots

Tasjao: dried beef jerk, food for enslaved people

Treaty of Tordesillas: a promise between Spain and Portugal not to invade certain countries

Vassal: a person who has protection and land from a ruler, in return for loyalty and service

Yerba mate: traditional herbal drink ritual

White man's burden: racist justification for white conquest which required patience because Africans were 'foolish, evil and childlike'

White man's privilege: natural and unrecognised benefits, rights or power, in society, organisations and industries for being born a white male

White saviour complex: white peoples' condescending attitude of 'saving or rescuing' Black peoples for their own emotional and /or career gains.

REFERENCES 1

Chapter 1
- New World Encyclopedia (2019) *Argentina*: https://www.newworldencyclopedia.org/p/index.php?title=Argentina&oldid=1020336.
- Kara D. Schultz (2015) The Kingdom of Angola is not Very Far from Here: The South Atlantic Slave Port of Buenos Aires, 1585–1640, *Slavery & Abolition*, 36:3, 424-444
- Worldometers.info (2020) *U.K. Population (Live)*: U.S.A: https://www.worldometers.info/world-population/uk-population/
- Time and date.com (2020) *Distance from London to…*: https://www.timeanddate.com/worldclock/distances.html?n=136
- Wikpedia.org (2020) *Symbols of Argentina*: https://en.wikipedia.org/wiki/National_symbols_of_Argentina
- Encyclopaedia Britannica contributors (2020) *Argentina:* Encyclopaedia Britannica. https://www.britannica.com/place/Argentina
- Claire Healy (2012) Argentina. In S. R. King: *Encyclopaedia of Free Blacks and People of Color in the Americas*
- Alex Borucki (2011) The Slave Trade to the Río de la Plata, 1777–1812: Trans-Imperial Networks and Atlantic Warfare, *Colonial Latin American Review*, 20:1, 81-107
- National Geographic, Caryl-Sue, Producer (2012) *South America: Physical Geography.* www.nationalgeographic.org/encyclopedia/south-america-physical-geography/
- WWF (2017) Promising rise in Jaguar Numbers in Argentina. *Good Nature Travel:* https://www.nathab.com/blog/promising-rise-in-jaguar-numbers-in-argentina/
- Mariana Altrichter and others (2006) The Decline of Jaguars Panthera onca in the Argentine Chaco: *Oryx,* v40(3) p. 302-309
- Iguazu National Park (n.d.) *World Heritage List*. UNESCO https://whc.unesco.org/en/list/303/
- Frederico Freitas (2015) The Guarani and the Iguaçu National Park. *ReVista (Cambridge),* 14(3), 18-22
- Frederico Freitas and others (2018) Argentinizing The Border: Conservation and Colonization in Iguazú National Park, 1890–1950 In *Big Water:* University of Arizona
- John Laundré and others (2001) Wolves, elk, and bison: the "landscape of fear" in Yellowstone National Park, USA. *Canadian Journal of Zoology*, 79(8) 1401-1409
- Jessica L Fort and others (2018) Factors influencing local attitudes and perceptions regarding jaguars Panthera onca …in Panama. *Oryx, 52*(2), 282–291

Chapter 2
- John Miaschi (World Atlas) (21 February 2018) Indigenous Peoples of Argentina: *Environment:* World Atlas
- Encyclopaedia Britannica (20 July 1998) *Diaguita:* Encyclopaedia Britannica, Inc: www.britannica.com/topic/Diaguita
- Evaldo Mendes da Silva (2018) Walking on the Bad Land in Jacob Blanc, Frederico Freitas (eds) *Big Water:* Tucson: University of Arizona Press.
- UNESCO (no date) *Cueva de las Manos, Río Pinturas: Description:* UNESCO: https://whc.unesco.org/en/list/936/
- Pedro Sarmiento de Gamboa. Quoted in Alfredo Prieto, Patagonian Painted Cloaks: An Ancient Puzzle, in *Patagonia: Natural History, Prehistory and Ethnography at the Uttermost End of the Earth* (1997) edited by Colin McEwan, Luis Borrero, and Alfredo Prieto, 173–85 (Princeton, NJ: Princeton University Press), 179
- Cambridge Encyclopedia (2002) *II.III.2 Hunter-Gatherers and the Colonial Encounter* in II.III Hunter-Gatherers in a global world
- Richard Hellie (2020) *Slavery Sociology*: Encyclopaedia Britannica: https://www.britannica.com/topic/slavery-sociology
- Jesuit Missions (Reducciones) (15 Jul 2020) *Encyclopedia of Latin American History and Culture.* Encyclopedia.com
- Bartolome de las Casas (25 April 2020) *History of the Indies* (1561): Wikiquote.org: https://en.wikiquote.org/wiki/Bartolom%C3%A9_de_las_Casas
- Julia J.S. Sarreal (2014) Bankruptcy: in *The Guaraní and Their Missions*: A Socioeconomic History. Stanford University Press
- Ralph H.Vigil (1971) *Negro Slaves and Rebels in the Spanish Possessions, 1503-1558*. The Historian (Kingston), v33 (4), p. 637-655

Chapter 3
- Joseph C. Miller (1976) *Kings and Kinsmen: Early Mbundu States in Angola*: Oxford: Clarendon Press.
- Christine Saidi (2016) *Kongo, Kingdom of: Encyclopedia of Empire*: editors John Mackenzie, Wiley 1st ed.
- Fikru Gebrekidan (2010) *Ethiopia and Congo: A Tale of Two Medieval Kingdoms*: Callaloo: V33, No. 1 Winter 2010, p 223-238; Johns Hopkins University Press
- Aurelien Gampiot and others. (2017) African Responses: The Birth of African Christianities: In Kimbanguism: An African Understanding of the Bible (pp. 34-61). Pennsylvania: Penn State University Press.
- Ras Michael Brown, Joan C. Bristol, Emily Suzanne Clark, Michael Pasquier, and two others (2014). Black Catholicism. *Journal of Africana Religions, 2*(2), 244-295.
- Fishery and Aquaculture (FAO.org) (2011) *Angola Country Profile Fact Sheets*; In FAO Fisheries and Aquaculture Department. Rome
- Guest Contributor (25 September 2019) Angola could become world's #1 diamond producer: Mining Review.com
- William Gervase and others (11 March 2020) *Angola*: Encyclopaedia Britannica Inc: https://www.britannica.com/place/Angola
- Nathan Nunn, Leonard Wantchekon (2011) *The Slave Trade and the Origins of Mistrust in Africa*: The American Economic Review, v101 (7) p. 3221-3252
- Nathan Nunn, Diego Puga (2012) *Ruggedness: The Blessing of Bad Geography in Africa*. The Review of Economics and Statistics, v94(1) p. 20–36
- Sarah Tishkoff, Scott Williams (2002) Genetic analysis of African populations: human evolution and complex disease. *Nat Rev Genet* 3, 611–621
- Herbert J Foster (1976) *Partners or Captives in Commerce? The Role of Africans in the Slave Trade*: Journal of Black Studies, v6(4) p. 421–434

REFERENCES 2

Chapter 3 contin...d
- Molefi Asante (2013) *Henry Louis Gates Is Wrong about African Involvement in the Slave Trade. Black and Brown News.* https://blackandbrownnews.com/molefi-kete-asante-henrylouis-gates-is-wrong-about-african-involvement-in-the-slave-trade.
- James Fenske, Kala Namrata (2015) Climate and the Slave Trade: *Journal of Development Economics*, v112. p. 19-32
- France Nkokomane Ntloedibe (2020) *Silencing Evidence: Reflections on the Scholarship on African Involvement in the European Slave Trade* African Historical Review
- France Nkokomane Ntloedibe (2018*) Revisiting modes of enslavement: the role of raiding, kidnapping and wars in the European slave trade* African Identities 16:3 349-364
- Walter Rodney (1981). *How Europe underdeveloped Africa.* Washington, DC: Howard University Press
- José Curto (2005) Resistencia à Escravidão na África: 1846-1876. *Afro-Ásia,33*. In R. Ferreira (2014) Slave Flights and Runaway Communities in Angola *Anos 90* (v21)40
- Enslaved with Samuel L Jackson*: A People Stolen* (2020) BBC2. Series 1. Varied Producers include Ric Esther Bienstock, Sarah Sapper and Felix Golubev
- Mariana Candido (2011) African Freedom Suits, Portuguese Vassal Status: Legal Mechanisms for Fighting Enslavement in Benguela Angola. *Slavery & Abolition* 32:3 447-459
- Samuel Haigh Esq (1831) *Sketches of Buenos Ayres, Chile, and Peru* (London: Effingham Wilson: Royal Exchange. https://archive.org/details/sketchesbuenosa01haiggoog
- Alex Borucki (2011) *The Slave Trade to the Río de la Plata,1777–1812*: Trans-Imperial Networks and Atlantic Warfare, Colonial Latin American Review, 20:1, 81-107
- Irene Diggs (1951) *The Negro in the Viceroyalty of the Río de la Plata:* The Journal of Negro History, v36 (no. 1/4) p. 281-281
- Kara D. Schultz (2015) *The Kingdom of Angola is not Very Far from Here. The Río de la Plata, Brazil, and Angola, 1580-1680.* http://hdl.handle.net/1803/15223
- Marina Muzzio and others (2018) Population structure in Argentina. *PLOS ONE* 13(5): e0196325
- Joseph C. Miller (1982) The Significance of Drought, Disease and Famine in the Agriculturally Marginal Zones of West-Central Africa *Journal of African History* v23(1)17–61
- Thomas Clarkson. Elizabeth Donnan (1930-1935) *Documents Illustrative of the History of the Slave Trade to America.* Published 1965
- Alexander Falconbridge (1788) *An account of the slave trade on the coast of Africa.* London: J. Phillips
- John Newton (1788) *Thoughts upon the African slave trade*: By John Newton. London: Printed for J. Buckland. Chicago
- Maghan Keita (2005) Middle passage. In M. K. Asante & A. Mazama (Eds.) *Encyclopedia of black studies* (p. 331-333) SAGE Publications, Inc.,
- Daniel Schavelzon (2014) On slaves and beer: the first images of the South Sea Company slave market in Buenos Aires, African and Black Diaspora: *An International Journal*

Chapter 4
- Tekla Ali Johnson (2004) *Colonial Caste Paradigms and The African Diaspora*, The Black Scholar, 34:1, 23-33
- Rebecca Earle (2016) *The Pleasures of Taxonomy: Casta Paintings, Classification, and Colonialism*: William & Mary Quarterly, v73(3) p. 427-466. Project MUSE
- Peter Wade (1993) *Blackness and Race Mixture: The Dynamics of Racial Identity in Colombia.* Johns Hopkins University Press. Series in Atlantic History and Culture
- Jack D Forbes (1990) *The Manipulation of Race, Caste and Identity: The evolution of Racism and Caste Terminology*: Journal of Ethnic Studies;17 4; SS Premium Collection 1
- Erika Edwards (2003) *Though Many Have White Skin, their Veins Flow of Black Blood*: Argentina: McNair Scholars Journal: v7: Iss. 1, Article 8.
- Douglas Richmond (2001) The Legacy of African Slavery in Colonial Mexico, 1519-1810 *Journal of Popular Culture*, v35(2) p 1-16.
- Agustin Parise (2008) *Slave Law and Labour Activities during the Spanish Colonial Period*: South American Region of Río de la Plata. Rutgers Law Record, 32, 1-30
- George Reid Andrews (1980) *The Afro-Argentines of Buenos Aires, 1800-1900*: University of Wisconsin Press, Madison, Wisconsin
- George Reid Andrews (1979) *Race versus Class Association: The Afro-Argentines of Buenos Aires, 1850-1900*: Journal of Latin American Studies, v11(1) p. 19–39
United Nations Human Rights (18 March 2019) Statement to the media by the United Nations Working Group of Experts on People of African Descent, on the conclusion of its official visit to Argentina: 11-18 March 2019 https://www.ohchr.org/EN/NewsEvents/Pages/DisplayNews.aspx?NewsID=24350&LangID=E

REFERENCES 3

Chapter 5
- Agustin Parise (2008) *Slave Law and Labour Activities during the Spanish Colonial Period*: South American Region of Río de la Plata. Rutgers Law Record, 32, 1-30
- Andrew Sluyter (2012) The Tasajo Trail. *In Black Ranching Frontiers: African Cattle Herders of the Atlantic World*, 1500-1900 p.169-210
- A. L. Lloyd (1951) Meat from Argentina: The History of a National Industry *History Today Online*, v1(3) p 30: www.historytoday.com/archive/meat-argentina-history-national-industry
- Thales A.Z. Pereira (2016) Was it Uruguay Or Coffee? The Causes of the Beef Jerky Industry's Decline in Southern Brazil (1850 - 1889) *Nova Economia* v26 (1) p.7-42.
- Arnold Strickon (1965) The Euro-American Ranching Complex: In A. Leeds Man, Culture and Animals: *The Role of Animals in Human Ecologica Adjustments*, 229–58
- George Reid Andrews (1980) *The Afro-Argentines of Buenos Aires, 1800-1900*: University of Wisconsin Press, Madison, Wisconsin
- Edward Telles, T. Paschel (2014) *Who Is Black, White, or Mixed Race? How Skin Color, Status, Nation Shape Racial Classification*. Journal of Sociology
- Samuel Haigh Esq (1831) *Sketches of Buenos Ayres, Chile, and Peru* (London: Effingham Wilson: Royal Exchange. https://archive.org/details/sketchesbuenosa01haiggoog
- Kara D. Schultz (2015) *The Kingdom of Angola is not Very Far from Here: The South Atlantic Slave Port of Buenos Aires, 1585–1640*, Slavery & Abolition, 36:3, 424-444
- Olaudah Equiano (1789) *The Interesting Narrative of the Life of Olaudah Equiano, or Gustavus Vassa, the African.* Second Edition, British Library

Chapter 6
- Alex Borucki (2017) *Across imperial boundaries: Black social networks across the Iberian South Atlantic, 1760-1810*: Atlantic Studies, v14 (1) p. 11-36
- Tekla Ali Johnson (2004) *Colonial Caste Paradigms and The African Diaspora*, The Black Scholar, 34:1, 23-33
- Schomburg Center for Research in Black Culture: New York Public Library: http://abolition.nypl.org/essays/african_resistance/3/
- Slave narratives: *Resistance and Rebellion*: Slavery and Remembrance.org.
- George Reid Andrews (1980) *The Afro-Argentines of Buenos Aires, 1800-1900*: University of Wisconsin Press, Madison, Wisconsin
- James Sidbury (1997) *Saint Domingue in Virginia*: Ideology, Local Meanings, and Resistance to Slavery, 1790- 1800. Journal of Southern History 63(3): 531–552
- Jeffrey R Kerr-Ritchie (2013) *Slave Revolt Across Borders*: Journal of African Diaspora Archaeology and Heritage, 2:1, 65-92
- Emily Berquist (2010) *Early Anti-Slavery Sentiment in the Spanish Atlantic World: 1765-1817*: Slavery & Abolition, v31 (2) p. 181-205
- Lyman L. Johnson (1979) *Manumission in Colonial Buenos Aires, 1776-1810*: The Hispanic American Historical Review, 59(2), 258-279
- United Nations Human Rights (18 March 2019) *Statement to the media by the United Nations Working Group of Experts on People of African Descent, on the conclusion of its official visit to Argentina: 11-18 March 2019* https://www.ohchr.org/EN/NewsEvents/Pages/DisplayNews.aspx?NewsID=24350&LangID=E
- Peter Blanchard (2014) *An Institution Defended: Slavery and the English Invasions of Buenos Aires in 1806-1807*. Slavery & Abolition, v35 (2) p. 253-272
- Magdalena Candioti (2019) *El tiempo de los libertos: conflictos y litigación en torno a la ley de vientre libre en el Río de la Plata ...* L História (São Paulo) 38, 14
- Casa Minima (no date) *The Complex. Discovering the origins of the city.* El Zanjón. http://www.elzanjon.com.ar/en

Chapter 7
- Seth Meisel (2003) From Slave to Citizen-Soldier in Early-Independence Argentina. *Historical Reflections / Réflexions Historiques*, 29(1), 65-82.
- Richard Gott (Friday 13 July 2007) Bad day for the empire: The *Guardian* News
- David Jays (Sunday 26 January 2020) The scandal of the £20bn bailout to slave-owning Brits: The *Guardian* News: Compensation: API Parliament Hansard 1818
- George Reid Andrews (1980) *The Afro-Argentines of Buenos Aires, 1800-1900*: University of Wisconsin Press, Madison, Wisconsin
- Emily Berquist (2010) Early Anti-Slavery Sentiment in the Spanish Atlantic World: 1765-1817: *Slavery & Abolition*, v31 (2) p. 181-205
- Juan Bautista Alberdi. *Argentina 1853 Constitution:* https://www.constituteproject.org/constitution/Argentina_1994.pdf?lang=en p. 7 Article 25, Article 75.18 and Article 12
- Simon Collier (1992). The Popular Roots of the Argentine Tango. *History Workshop*, (34), 92-100.
- Cyril Hamshere (1971) *The British In Argentina:* History Today Ltd, London: https://www.historytoday.com/archive/british-argentina
- David Rock (2008) *The British in Argentina: From Informal Empire to Postcolonialism*. Bulletin of Latin American Research, 27: 49-77
- Daniel Schávelzon (2013) *Argentina and Great Britain: Studying an Asymmetrical Relationship through Domestic Material Culture*: Hist. Archaeology, v47(1) p. 10-25
- Carlos Sarasola (2010) *The Conquest of the Desert and the Free Indigenous Communities of the Argentine Plains*. Chapter in Military Struggle and Identity Formation
- Amy K. Kaminsky (2008) *The Race for National Identity: In Argentina*: Stories for a Nation, 99-121. Minneapolis; London: University of Minnesota Press
- Rory Carroll (Thursday 13 January 2011) Argentinian founding father recast as genocidal murderer: The *Guardian* Newspaper: Courtesy of Guardian News & Media Ltd

REFERENCES 4

Chapter 8
- George Reid Andrews (1980) *The Afro-Argentines of Buenos Aires, 1800-1900*: University of Wisconsin Press, Madison, Wisconsin
- Miriam Gomes Service – Interview with Ruthie Ackerman (27 November 2005) *Blacks in Argentina -- officially a few, but maybe a million*: Chronicle Foreign
- Erika Edwards (2014) Mestizaje, Córdoba's patria chica: beyond the myth of black disappearance in Argentina. *African and Black Diaspora: An International Journal*, 7:2,89-104
- Florencia Guzmán (2016) Maria Remedios del Valle "The Captain", "Mother of the Nation" and "Girl Ayohuma". New World Debates Journals Open Edition.org
- Ministry of Culture Argentina (no date) *Participate to recognize the figure of María Remedios del Valle*. https://www.cultura.gob.ar/maria-remedios-del-valle-valiente-capitana-9620/
- United Nations Human Rights (18 March 2019) Statement to the media by the United Nations Working Group of Experts on People of African Descent, on the conclusion of its official visit to Argentina: 11-18 March 2019 https://www.ohchr.org/EN/NewsEvents/Pages/DisplayNews.aspx?NewsID=24350&LangID=E
- Peter Blanchard (2014) *An Institution Defended: Slavery and the English Invasions of Buenos Aires in 1806-1807*. Slavery & Abolition, v35 (2) p. 253-272
- M. F. Mantilla (1889) Los negros argentinos. El monumento a Falucho Revista Nacional. In Seth Meisel (2003) *From Slave to Citizen-Soldier in Early-Independence Argentina*: Historical Reflections / Réflexions Historiques 29, no. 1: 65-82
- Felix Colon y Larraitegui's legal handbook (1788) *The Military Courts of Spain and Its Indies* (1778) In Seth Meisel (2003) From Slave to Citizen-Soldier in Early-Independence Argentina. Historical Reflections / Réflexions Historiques, 29(1), 65-82.
- Bartolome Mitre 'Falucho' (1940-1956) Phylon 5, no. 2 (1944): 136-37: Clark Atlanta University Argentina: *Historical Reflections / Réflexions Historiques* 29(1) 65-82
- Donald S. Castro (1994) *The Afro-Argentine Payador Tradition: The Art of Gabino Ezeiza*. Afro-Hispanic Review, 13(2), 9-17

Chapter 9
- Irene Diggs (1951) *The Negro in the Viceroyalty of the Río de la Plata*: The Journal of Negro History, v36 (no. 1/4) p. 281-281
- Nestor Ortiz Oderigo (1969) *Calunga, croquis del candombe*. Buenos Aires: Editorial Universitaria de Buenos Aires
- The UNESCO Courier (1977) *Latin America: composite profile of a continent*: p. 60-63
- Matthew B Karush, (2012) *Blackness in Argentina: Jazz, Tango and Race before Peron*. Past & Present, no. 216, p. 215–245
- Sarah Quesada (2015) *An Inclusive 'Black Atlantic': Revisiting Historical Creole Formations:* Latin American and Caribbean Ethnic Studies, 10:2, p.226-246,
- Alfredo Zitarros *in* The UNESCO Courier (1977) *Latin America: composite profile of a continent*: p. 60-63
- Donald S. Castro (1994) *The Afro-Argentine Payador Tradition: The Art of Gabino Ezeiza*. Afro-Hispanic Review, 13(2), 9-17
- George Reid Andrews (1980) *The Afro-Argentines of Buenos Aires, 1800-1900*: University of Wisconsin Press, Madison, Wisconsin
- Alex Borucki (2018) *From Colonial Performers to Actors of American Liberty*: Black Artists in Bourbon and Revolutionary …, v75 (2) p. 261-289. Project MUSE
- Anahi Viladrich (2013) *More Than Two to Tango: Argentine Tango Immigrants in New York City.* University of Arizona Press.
- A. L. Lloyd (1951) Meat from Argentina: The History of a National Industry: *History today Online*, v1(3) p.30 www.historytoday.com/archive/meat-argentina-history-national-industry
- Charles Darwin in Andrew Sluyter (2012) *The Tasajo Trail. In Black Ranching Frontiers*: African Cattle Herders of the Atlantic World, 1500-1900(p.169-210. Yale
- Andrew Sluyter (2012) *The Pampas. In Black Ranching Frontiers*: African Cattle Herders of the Atlantic World, 1500-1900: Yale University Press:
- Angle Flores, Norman Thomas di Giovanni (1942) El Matadero: Esteban Echeverria: *New Mexico Quarterly* 12, 4. (1809-1851) https://digitalrepository.unm.edu/nmq/vol12/iss4/3
- Encyclopedia Britannica (November 30, 2018) *Yerba Mate:* https://www.britannica.com/topic/mate-beverage
- Adalberto López (1974) The Economics of Yerba Mate in Seventeenth-Century South America. *Agricultural History*, 48(4), 493-509.
- United Nations (11 January 2017) International Convention on the Elimination of All Forms of Racial Discrimination CERD/C/ARG/CO/21-23: https://www.ohchr.org/EN/Countries/LACRegion/Pages/ARIndex.aspx
- United Nations (1 November 2018) Economic and Social Council. E/C.12/ARG/CO/4: https://www.ohchr.org/EN/Countries/LACRegion/Pages/ARIndex.aspx
- United Nations (11-18 March 2019) Statement to the media by the United Nations Working Group of Experts on People of African Descent on the conclusion of its official visit to Argentina. Buenos Aires: https://www.ohchr.org/EN/NewsEvents/Pages/DisplayNews.aspx?NewsID=24350&LangID=E

PICTURE CREDITS

Front cover: flag/ad_krikorian: ivory coast slaves/ilbusca: istock.com; Back cover flag: Алексей Бутенков/123rf.com

Figure 1	World map continents/Pixabay 27406
Figure 2	Argentina Map/CC Maphill.com
Figure 3	Continental Drift Pangea/TCU IdeaFactory
Figure 4	Río de la Plata from the sky/WikiPictures
Figure 5	Buenos Aires 1860/The New York Public Library
Figure 6	Río de la Plata maps/CC Wikimedia
Figure 7	Map of Regions & Provinces/andescampers.com
Figure 8	Flag of Argentina/PD Wikimedia
Figure 9	Argentina coat of arms/PD Wikimedia
Figure 10	Erythrina crista-galli/Kurt Stueber, Wikimedia
Figure 11	Regions in Argentina/Realworldholidays.co.uk
Figure 12	Gauchos on the Pampas/Taringa.net
Figure 13	Alpine tundra/Bjørn Christian@ Wikimedia
Figure 14	Iguazu Falls/Goodfreephotos.com
Figure 15	Jaguars face threats/San Diego Shooter Flickr
Figure 16	Guarani women/Nastasic iStockphoto.com
Figure 18	Patagonians giants/ De Neuville's Iroquois Drawings
Figure 19	Cave of Hands/Mariano/PD Wikimedia
Figure 20	Spain gave up trading rights/PD Wikimedia
Figure 21	How the Indians Collect Gold/Bridgeman.co.uk
Figure 22	Mother and Daughter/PD Wikimedia
Figure 23	General view of reduction/historiasanignacio.com.ar
Figure 24	San Ignacio Mini/ Pablo Flores Flickr
Figure 25	Carte d'Afrique 1745/Guillaume Delisle Wikimedia
Figure 26	King of Kongo/Thomas Astley, Slavery Images
Figure 27	Kimpa Vita Beatriz/PD Wikimedia
Figure 28	Capital city of Angola/Bruno Madeira Pixabay
Figure 29	Fish market/Carsten ten Brink, Flickr
Figure 30	The Assiento/Slavery and Remembrance.org
Figure 31	Gun only/CC International Slavery Museum
Figure 32	Olaudah Equiano/CC British Library
Figure 33	Brookes slave ship/PD Wikimedia
Figure 34	Account of Sales/NY Historical Society Museum
Figure 35	Page 2 Account of Sales/NY Historical Society Museum
Figure 36	European conquest/DarkmoonArt_de Pixabay
Figure 37	Origin of 133/Kara D Schultz (2015) (see refs)
Figure 38	Black for sale without defects /www. abc.es/ historia/abci-vende-negra-sin-defectosabc.es
Figure 39	Spanish Racial Pyramid/adapted from Sutori.com
Figure 40	Spanish man and Black Woman/CC Cristóbal Lozano
Figure 41	*Casta* Painting/Ignacio María Barreda, PD Wikimedia
Figure 42	De Español y Mestiza/Miguel Cabrera Wikimedia
Figure 43	Typical *Casta*/in Rebecca Earle (2016) see refs
Figure 44	Andrés de Islas, De Español, y Alvina/Wikimedia
Figure 45	From Spanish and Black/PD Wikimedia
Figure 46	Slavery in chains/Gustavo La Rotta Amaya, Flickr
Figure 47	Ostrich Hunting/Bridgeman.co.uk
Figure 48	Painting of Gauchos/Taringa.net
Figure 49	Gauchos hunting/Ayay Wallpapers
Figure 50	Cross section of early water lifting/www.fao.org/
Figure 51	Tasajo/Rebeca Cruz Gavlan, Pixabay
Figure 52	Cutting Sugar Cane Museum/Natalia A, Tripadvisor
Figure 53	The Sellers/See image caption on page 44
Figure 54	Enslaved Domestic/See image caption on page 45
Figure 55	Numbers of children/Kara D. Schultz (2015) see refs
Figure 56	Africans fought/New York Public Library
Figure 57	A Ride for Liberty painting/Steven Zucker, Flickr
Figure 58	Representation of an Insurrection …/PD
Figure 59	Black man being whipped/Slavery Images.org
Figure 60	Code Noir of 1742/Selbymay CC Wikipedia
Figure 61	Burning of the town/Archives Charmet. Bridgeman
Figure 62	Manumission by Slave/Yale University
Figure 63	Two iron shackles /PD www.lookandlearn.com
Figure 64	La Casa Mínima/CC Wikimedia
Figure 65	Colourful houses/Lea Limbruner, Pixabay
Figure 66	British invasions 1744/PD Wikimedia
Figure 67	Portrait of Colonel Lorenzo/PD Wikimedia
Figure 68	Slavery statue/PD Wikiwand
Figure 69	Western Europe/Freeworldmaps.net
Figure 70	Patagonian Indians/Heritage Images, Alamy
Figure 71	Old Patagonian/Gustavo Perretto, Wikimedia
Figure 72	Tren a las nubes / Casa Rosada, Wikimedia
Figure 73	Slavery in 1529/Christoph Weiditz PD
Figure 74	Very Black/Afropunk
Figure 75	What's it like to be black/BBC video screen
Figure 76	Maria Remedios/Televisión Pública Argentina
Figure 77	Monument/Black Falucho Gutenberg.org
Figure 78	Candombe painting/Pedro Figari, Alamy
Figure 79	Candombe. Impressionist by Pedro Figari/Alamy
Figure 80	Two Tango dancers in black and red/123rf.com
Figure 81	Pulperias/Enrique McGrech@ CC ECyT-ar
Figure 82	Gabino Ezeiza – A Payador/Todotango.com
Figure 83	Los Chinchulines cow intestines/Abrasados CC
Figure 84	Engraving…Saladero 1880s/Chapel Hill Libraries
Figure 85	Tomado Mate:/New York Public Library
Figure 86	1841 The Governor of …/D de Plott, PD Wikimedia
Figure 87	Author photo/Zakariya Gayle

PD= public domain
CC=creative commons

QUOTE CREDITS / PRIMARY SOURCES

1. 1561/Bartolomé de las Casas Wikiquote
2. 1522/http://www.wright.edu/~christopher.oldstone-moore/Casas.htm
3. 1526 letter/https://genius.com/Nzinga-mbemba-afonso-i-letters-to-the-king-of-portugal-1526-annotated
4. Kimpa Vita/Cecile Fromont (2014-11-24) Art of Conversion: Christian Visual Culture in the Kingdom of Kongo. University of North Carolina Press.
5. 1730/Dutch Director General Rademacher Arch Elmina No. 596 Short Memoir
6. Olaudah Equiano 1789/British Library
7. 1787/Thomas Clarkson: Babel.hathitrust.org
8. 1788/Alexander Falconbridge: Babel.hathitrust.org
9. 1788 John Newton/Cowper & Newton Museum.Org. uk
10. 1730s/From A Short Account of the African Slave Trade by Robert Norris: https://docsouth.unc.edu/neh/norris/norris.html p 171
11. 1730s/Ship's log Captain Robert/Liverpool Museum
33. Account of Sales of the Ascensions Cargo of Slaves and Buenos Ayres
12. from Maxine Hanon. *In* D. Schavelzon (2014) see refs
13. 1774/Excerpt from Dn. Pedro Alonso O'Crouley, Description of the Kingdom of New Spain translated by Seán Dublin: Allen Figgis 1972
14. 1829/Return of British Trade Consulate of Buenos http://www.argbrit.org/BAport/movements1829.htm
15. 1884/Ricardo Pillado (1906). Politica Comercial Argentina. Buenos Aires
16. 1791/An abstract of evidence delivered before a select Committee Narratives from the Collection on Resistance and Rebellion. Recovered histories.org
17. 1818/ https://api.parliament.uk/historic- hansard commons1818/jan/28/copy-of-the-treaty-with-spain-for
18. 1878/Excerpt Conquest of the Desert speech Wikimedia
19. 1855/Military officer and governor of provinces/journals.openedition.org
20. 1812-1818/Extract from Black Troops Regiment of Freeman
21. 1778/Felix Colon https://digitalcollections.nypl.org/items /510d4db-c487-a3d9-e040-e00a18064a99
22. 1889/Los Negroes Argentinos by Manuel J Mantilla New Mexico. Quarterly 12(4) (1809-1851 https://digitalcollections.nypl.org/items/6e696c30-da2a-0132-bdce-58d385a7b928
23. 1809/El Matadero (The Slaughterhouse) by Esteban Esteban Echeverria (1809) quoted in Angle Flores (1942) New Mexico quarterly

INDEX

admixtures 35-36
Afro-Argentine iv, 55, 70, 77, 82
Angola iv, 1, 17, 19-24, 27, 29, 48, 75-76
    kidnap 12, 14, 17, 21-24, 64
    Kongo iv, 1, 14, 17-19, 23, 28-29, 75-76
Assiento 20, 24, 29, 38
aquí no hay negroes iv, 50, 56, 69-70, 76

barrio 28, 57, 76-77
    Cordoba 32
    La Boca 57, 76
    San Telmo 28, 57, 59, 68, 76-77
    Tucumán 45, 47
blackness v, 32-37, 71
blanqueamiento 69, 73
    skin colour 13, 22, 32, 39, 56
    whitened 42, 76
    whiteness v, 18, 32-34, 39
Brazil 1, 3, 6-7, 12, 14, 27, 44, 48, 61
Britain 11, 20-21, 29, 38, 53, 61-66
    British 20, 23, 27-29, 44, 52-53, 57, 59, 61, 63, 66

Casas, Bartolomé de las 13, 15
chattel slavery 22, 25-26, 30, 53
children 32-34, 39, 40, 47-48, 53, 55, 68-69
Constitution 63-64, 66
Conquest of the Desert 10, 64, 66

disappearance iv, 50, 63, 68-69, 73, 76
    erased 4, 43-44, 70-71

Eurocentric iv, 14, 17, 21-24, 29-30, 42, 51-52, 68, 75
European slave trade v, 18-19, 22, 44, 62
Equiano, Olaudah 22, 30

Freedom Womb Act 56, 62

gaucho 5, 11, 13, 42-43, 48, 50, 75, 77-79
Gracias al Sacar 34
guns 17, 20-24, 29

Iberia 11-12, 15, 20, 32-33
invaders 2, 5, 7, 9-11, 15, 19-20, 52, 72
    conquistador iv, 2, 4, 11-12, 15

Kimpa Vita (Dona Beatriz) 18, 29

Luso African 21, 24, 27
    see mixed-race
    see Sistema de Casta
limpieza de sangre 32
L'Ouverture, Toussaint 54, 58
Haiti Revolution 18, 54, 58, 61

manumission 4, 52-55, 58-59, 75
middle passage 22-24, 33, 37, 53, 63, 76
military 6, 10, 18, 42, 61, 68, 70-72, 80
    El Negro Falucho 71-73
    Maria Remedios Del Valle 70,73
misappropriation 43, 48, 57, 76, 79
mixed-race 13, 23, 32-35, 40, 53, 56

national symbols 4, 7
historia negra negada iv, 1,42-44, 54, 57, 63, 71, 76
Indian people iv, 1-6, 9-15, 27, 32-36, 64-66, 79-80
    Guarani speakers 1, 4, 6, 9, 11,14, 79, 80

Pampas 5-6, 11, 13, 42-43, 64, 75
Patagonia 3-5, 9-11, 15, 64-65
payadores 42, 75, 77, 80
peon 13, 42, 45

Piezas de Indias 38-40, 47
Portugal 11, 14, 17, 20, 32, 38
Portuguese iv, 1, 12, 17-23, 27, 29, 50, 52, 63, 76

racism 22, 32, 34, 39, 46, 68-69, 73, 77, 2
    discrimination 32, 46, 55, 70, 72, 82
    prejudice 32, 39
    stereotype 9, 15, 32, 35, 37, 43, 50, 58, 64, 71-72
racist v, 34, 36, 52, 70, 78, 82
Reducciones 14, 79
    Encomienda 12-15, 45
    Jesuits 14-15, 57, 79
Resistance 50-52

servitude iv, 22
silver 1, 2, 4, 7, 11-12, 28, 79
Sistema de Casta 32-35, 39, 53
    see blanqueamiento
    see mixed-race
slaughterhouse 2, 12, 44, 78
sold 17, 23-28, 30, 42, 44, 46, 56, 61-62,71-73

tango 52, 75-77, 80
    candombe 52, 75-76, 80
    milonga 75-76, 80
Treaty of Friendship, Navigation, and Commerce 63
Treaty of Paris 61
Treaty of Tordesillas 11, 14, 20

UNESCO 5-7, 10, 14, 75-76
United Nations 19, 38, 55, 59, 68, 70, 82

wealth gap, racial 44
    intergenerational wealth gap 32, 44, 56, 63
white man's burden 52, 55-56, 58, 62
white saviour complex 53, 62

AUTHOR

Figure 87: Author photo by Zakariya Gayle.

Pamela Gayle was born in South London, England, United Kingdom, from Jamaican parents. She gained a Bachelor of Education Honours degree, and majored in Humanities; an MA in Anthropology, where her thesis was entitled 'Searching for Roots in the Gambia'. More recently, Pamela gained a PGDip distinction in Environmental Studies.

Pamela has taught in primary schools for over 25 years, with additional responsibilities as Black History Manager. As early as 2002, Pamela implemented Black History Month for every month of the year. Due to the lack of Black resources in the UK at that time, she went on a fact-finding mission to the Black Arts Festival in Atlanta, USA. Pamela returned with the enough resources to implement Black History across every age and year groups for every month of the year. This was a great success, and won the local authority's Schools Black History competition.

Pamela's passion is travelling to sites of Black interest, history, and culture, and learning about the Black history that she was never taught at school. She has indulged her wandering spirit by participating in teacher exchange schemes abroad. One year was spent on the Commonwealth Teachers scheme to Trinidad and Togabo. She also spent another year on the USA Fulbright teaching scheme to California and later on, taught English in Spain. On return, she participated in various short-term teacher exchanges to Europe, via the British Council. Pamela also won a grant from Goldsmiths company (who are currently researching their own links to the European slave trade), to carry out her own personal research in Cuba, entitled Sugar, Slavery and Spanish.

Pamela still lives in South London. She would love a cat, but travels too much to look after one. Cycling, chocolate, dub reggae, salsa and yoga, are her hobbies, but not at the same time – and not necessarily in that order! This is Pamela's first book as an independent author. If you liked this book, please consider leaving feedback and suggestions.

Watch out for her next Black History Truth book.

Pamela Gayle

www.ingramcontent.com/pod-product-compliance
Lightning Source LLC
Chambersburg PA
CBHW041952150426

43197CB00004B/98